THE FLIGHT OF THE FEATHERED SERPENT

Armando Cosani

First published in Spanish language as:
"El Vuelo de la Serpiente Emplumada"

First edition 1953, Ediciones Sol
Sixth edition 1993, Editora y Distribuidora Yug, S.A., Mexico

This translation Copyright © 2003 by Patricia Atkinson and Edith Pritchard
First Edition, October 2003   ISBN: 0-9740560-2-2

All rights reserved. No part of this book may be reproduced or transmitted in any form or by any means without permission in writing from the copyright holders.

Published by Absolute Publishing LLC
39270 Paseo Padre Pkwy, PMB #327
Fremont, CA 94538, USA
Email: info@absolutepublishing.net
Website: www.absolutepublishing.net

Book Design by Patricia Atkinson

Printed in United States of America

Library of Congress Control Number: 2003112480

"The first Word of God sounded where there was no heaven or earth. And it detached itself from his Stone and fell to the second time and declared his divinity. And all the immensity of the eternal shook. And his word was a measure of grace, a glimpse of grace and broke and hollowed the spine of the mountains. Who was born when he came down? Great Father, You know it.

His first Principle was born and bore the spine of the mountains. Who was born there? Who? Father, You know it. It was born he who is tender in heaven."

Book of the Spirits, Code of
CHILAM BALAM DE CHUYAMEL

"And as Moses lifted up the serpent in the wilderness, even so must the Son of man be lifted up:

That whosoever believeth in him should not perish, but have eternal life.

For God so loved the world, that he gave his only begotten Son, that whosoever believeth in him should not perish, but have everlasting life."

SAINT JOHN III 14-16

First Book	*7*
Second Book	*111*
Third Book	*155*
Glossary	*207*

First Book

1

I could never understand this strange man of moderate words, who seemed to enjoy confusing me with his caustic and paradoxical observations upon all things. He gave the impression of being taciturn. However, soon after dealing with him, one couldn't help but notice the most extraordinary fact that I have come across in my agitated life: he was a smile. He was a smile from head to toe. He didn't smile, he didn't need to smile; he was that smile all over. This impression reached me in a very curious manner and it is difficult to explain. I will only say that smiling seemed to be a natural property of his body and that it emanated even from his way of walking. I never heard him laughing, but he had the gift of communicating his happiness or his seriousness depending on the situation. I never saw him depressed or upset, not even during those turbulent days towards the end of the Second World War, where as a consequence of a political revolution, I ended up in prison. He did absolutely nothing to obtain my freedom. Even in this incident, he showed to be a man out of the ordinary. He even seemed to be determined that I continue under arrest, and once upon a time when I condemned such an attitude, he said to me:

"You are better off here than out there. At least here you are in good company and it is even possible that you wake up."

"But here you can't even sleep," I said.

"That is what you think because you don't know yet which of the ways of sleeping is more dangerous and harmful in the long term. There is someone who watches over you even when you sleep and you are in good company."

In the ward where I was under arrest, there were also many men, whose intellectual values I respected and whose conversations were interesting to me. I used to play endless games of chess with some of them. However, our chat always went towards the political events that ended with our imprisonment. I made my friend see this one afternoon when he came to visit me with Christmas presents.

"You are still asleep" was his whole answer.

That day we talked for a good while and it occurred to me to ask him:

"How is it that you come to visit me so often and you haven't disappeared like the others who fled as soon as they knew about my situation?"

"I am more than a friend; I am the friendship that unites us."

I couldn't help smiling, with it I wanted to tell him that it wasn't the right time to throw his paradoxes at me and I insisted:

"But, how is it that the police haven't arrested you knowing you are my most intimate friend?"

His answer was as incomprehensible as everything else:

"Friendship protects me. And it protects you too, although in a different way."

And after an instant of silence he added:

"You do not understand me because you still depend on them in the same way that they depend on you. Neither you nor them depend on yourselves yet, although all of you are convinced of the opposite. If only you could understand this, you would understand everything else in its own time."

This stirred me up and I answered violently; saying that his words were very interesting like philosophy in nights of boredom. However in the circumstances I was in they became unbearable nonsense.

"Besides," I added so worked up and using terms impossible to publish, "how can I depend on them? The only thing they are useful for is to lick the boots of that petty dictator. Or perhaps I also depend on any idiot who supports himself with an army and exaggerates his popularity while he has the opposition gagged. Do I also depend on those who pursue intelligence and speak of progress? I wouldn't be surprised if you told me this now."

He looked at me with his invariable and patient smile. He listened until I was finished and offering me cigarettes and a light, he answered:

"You said it. You also depend on him and upon many other things. These," he made a gesture meaning the armed guards who were on the other side of the bars, "support him with their guns because they can't do anything else but obey the one who knows how to order them. Without weapons, without uniforms and without leaders they wouldn't be anything. They believe themselves to be the owners of their weapons, but the reality is that they are slaves of them. However, you and the ones who are arrested here are worse. These ones wear uniforms because they are afraid to walk alone in life, and because they can't do anything more productive for the world. They also wear a uniform in their heads. But you are worse. You say that you are men of intellect but in reality you are fools and in love with your foolishness. You support this dictatorship and whatever other dictatorship there is. You support them much better and more efficiently than the others. Your support takes place in many ways, but mainly by means of your stupid pride that makes you live with your back to the truth. And not only do you support it, but you strengthen it. Yes, you are worse than those who are honestly ignorant. However, none of you are really guilty."

He said all this to me so calmly and seriously that I was speechless. A good while went past before I asked him:

"What is it that we ignore?"

"A very simple fact that is really a physical truth but that you all believe to be just an ethical rule, impossible to put into practice. Surely, you have read it or heard it sometime: Do not resist evil."

"All these precepts were given to the world by authentic wise men. Only a handful of beings in the history of humanity have been able to discover that they are in fact scientific truths. Certainly, ordinary science will deny this because it believes that ethics are something separate from what it calls matter, without noticing that it is precisely what conditions and enlivens matter and even creates its forms.

A long time ago, there was a true wise man amongst men of science called Mesmer. Science, or that which they call science, persecuted him and all his work has been ignored. This is the destiny of those who discover the truth. Today mesmerism is like a form of charlatanism. And the curious thing is that it is precisely the charlatans of science who rattle on against Mesmer's *charlatanism.*

Those few who have studied Mesmer in order to carry out magnetic healing have come closer to the truth that he left hidden in his aphorisms. But only a few, very few, have noticed that which is *yes* can also be *no*. That *yes* is a relative truth to *no*, just as *good* is relative to *bad*. But you will have the opportunity to know this because at last you have asked me something worthwhile."

I must confess that the words of this friend always seemed crazy to me. That afternoon he left happier and more satisfied than usual, promising me another visit in a couple of days, which according to the regulations of the prison was extremely difficult. When I made the observation, he said:

"You know how to ride a bicycle, don't you?"

"Naturally," I said.

"Good. Those who know how to ride their own bicycle can ride any other."

What the hell has a bicycle got to do with his visit? Often I asked myself this and many other questions arising from his words.

I'm still asking myself this question without finding an adequate answer. I must also confess that reason pointed out to me that this man was crazy, however I felt a singular affection towards him.

I wanted to represent him like this, acting in an important event of my life. In that event, which marked the end of a career to which I had given all my strength and all my enthusiasm. It was truly a hard blow I suffered when I lost the position I conquered after long years of painful work. However, when I said all these things to my friend, he limited himself to responding:

"It is the best that could have happened to you. Now it only depends on you that your own awakening doesn't cause you greater suffering."

Then he told me many things, which at the time I took as words he used to comfort me, insisting that I possessed certain personal qualities that indicated a promising awakening.

Certainly, this account doesn't aim to be an autobiography, neither to detail the particulars of my hectic existence before and after this event. And if I have to record some personal facts it is because I need to give some background to explain my friend, and also to back up the writings that he asked me to publish at this time "with the aim of increasing the number of ours."

I remember that every time I asked him what he meant by ours, and who they were, he responded:

"A very special kind of bee that occurs only from time to time and with great efforts."

This was my friend's will, and I'm carrying it out, not only because I gave my word, but because I notice something in all this that might have some value which escapes me. It is possible that one of the readers knows what it is all about, and could perhaps explain this man to me.

It is also necessary that I make a confession: I don't know his name, he never told me his real name, and, except once, it never occurred to me to ask him those rigorous questions that demand name and surname, age, nationality, profession, etc.

Perhaps one of you knows him or has had news about him. And I say this because, in that occasion where I wanted to raise this aspect of his being, I let him glimpse my interest towards his origin and the rest of the things he never explained spontaneously; unlike any other man who does this to inspire trust in others. My friend was very different to the all the people I have met in my life, and it seemed he didn't care what impression he made. So when the question was raised about my interest for his identity, he said these enigmatic words:

"Those who truly want can know me. It is only necessary to want it to commence. I am everywhere in general and nowhere in particular. To those who call me I come. But this is only a way of saying it, because the reality is another. Few know how to call me; and it usually happens that when I come to them, they get frightened and overwhelm me with many questions: Who are you? What's your name? What do you live off? What's your job? Something along those lines, I never answer to this kind of impertinence because if a man doesn't know what he wants, it's best that he doesn't know anything about me either. It also happens that those who look for me without realising either decide not to pay any attention to me, or claim everything for themselves. There are also those who consider me *bad*. However this is only natural in this age of true degeneration of the human intelligence. I ruin people's dreams, not leaving one of their illusions up. Few decide to keep in contact with me; however these few are truly fortunate because they have the opportunity to know the true value of life. It is clear that this knowledge has its responsibilities; but you will get to know this at the appropriate time."

I remember that, in that occasion I said to him.

"Then I'm very glad I haven't bothered you. I beg you to forgive my curiosity. I wouldn't want to lose contact with you for anything in the world."

After these words, he smiled and added:

"There is a simple way to keep in contact with me: remembering. Remembrance is the link with the memory. In the memory resides the knowledge or the truth. To unite from the heart to the truth is what is transcendental. Enjoy my friendship while I'm with you. It will be useful for you to try to understand and comprehend the things I tell you. All efforts you make in this respect will be a positive gain for you, even when it often seems to you that all your life is falling apart. You are one of those who have called me without fully realising that you were looking for me. You haven't overwhelmed me with questions or with foolish requests. However, I must warn you that even though you have some qualities that keep me by your side, these same qualities can move me completely away from you, if you don't wake up. At least, if you were to wake up now, and this is entirely up to you, you won't suffer what you would with certainty have to suffer when you ought to remain alone and in silence, like in the desert. I can only accompany you for some time. If you don't learn how to treasure what I give you, it would only be your fault."

At that time, it bothered me the protective tone he used to talk to me in these cases. His seriousness seemed to me absurd and out of place. Many friends and some of my work mates felt a noticeable antipathy towards him. They asked me what did I see in this friend and they described him as an odd character; some of them said that he didn't have feelings, that nothing moved him. But I know he was a man full of love. When I commented on my friends' opinions due to a social incident, he said to me:

"Don't let those opinions worry you. They are the scum of humanity, the true evil of society. You will always find in their pockets the thirty pieces of silver. I have nothing with them, nothing do I want to have. They are subjected to other forces from which they could free themselves if they would really want to, but they have fallen in love with themselves, and confuse feelings with their personal weaknesses."

But it will be best and more practical if I do a chronological description of the events.

2

I got into journalism because after one of the many wars of this century, I remained with one of my legs so badly damaged that it was impossible for me to resume my profession in mercantile marine. The fact that I knew some languages and could translate Morse code and that I didn't write all that bad, were factors that helped me in this enterprise. I was ambitious, and wanted to make a career because I felt very vividly that my health was working against me, and that years were becoming shorter each time. I renounced the adventures and pleasure that traveling without direction gives, like when I enrolled as crewmember in any ship, in any port. I also renounced poetry and many other things that until now had cheered my existence. It was unpleasant to walk leaning on a stick, and it was even more unpleasant to have to sometimes resort to crutches. I didn't have the money needed for a specialist to treat my leg properly, and I had run away frightened from my country in view of the little maternal protection from military hospitals. I had well founded reasons for that. I had seen too many things. However, this doesn't have anything but the value of a personal background.

The salary I was earning was minimal. I worked with enthusiasm and eagerness to prosper. I not only wanted to make a career and create a name for myself in journalism, but I was also realising that, as long as I was relying one day on a stick, and the next one on crutches – depending on the human density of the trams I had to catch to and back from work - my possibilities in life were limited to be a translator and nothing else. My first objective was then to earn money. And, since I have by heritage and by education, certain religious ideas, I thought that the best thing would be to ask for help from heaven. I thought to make my petitions to some of the saints to whom they attribute miracles, but my work acted against that decision. The news covered information about the world situation on the verge of the Second World War and about that regrettable comedy of puppets in Geneva. These acted powerfully over my spirit and ended undermining my belief in saints. I couldn't explain to myself how it was possible that with so much prayer, with so many diligent petitions to the saints, the world continued to be involved in an orgy of blood, which I had experienced in my own flesh, and about which my stick and crutches spoke eloquently. Without the need of its truth to be corroborated by the sharp pains I used to suffer. In the middle of all this, I consoled myself thinking that I still had my leg and that I had a possibility to save it. Others ended up worse than me, they had lost either legs or arms with injuries of much less importance than mine.

All this, apart from other too intimate things, determined my intention in such a way that I left aside the idea of asking for monetary help to Saint Judas Tadeo, or Saint Pancrasio, or to any of the other saints who, in theory and in accordance with religious propaganda, usually perform miracles. I decided to present my troubles directly and personally to Our Lord Jesus Christ. After all, I always felt that My Lord Jesus Christ, as well as Hail Mary moved me powerfully. And that's how I started to go around several temples in search of an adequate environment, until I found one where there was a beautiful painting of The Heart of Jesus, which dominated the altar and the central nave.

But, at this stage, it is necessary that I confess, that I had given up attending mass on Sundays and Public Holidays because, in those days, I preferred to stay in bed at the modest bed-sit where I had a room so I could give my leg a good rest. Besides, I had a guilty conscience. I considered the holy sacraments to be banned from me forever. This had its origin in the war. I had a violent clash with the chaplain of my unit when, desperately, I told him that I thought God was rubbish and that I didn't understand how it was possible that, through his ministers he allowed such slaughtering of youngsters. This incident happened after a mass on the battlefront, on the eve where several hundreds of young men, between 16 and 18 years old, received their baptism of fire. The chaplain had offered me communion saying: "just in case you die." This caused me such repugnance that I violently emptied over him all the anger I had accumulated within during one year of living in a shirt teeming with lice, without water and going through hunger. I am a violent man, and back then I pressed the trigged easily, as if the most natural function of life was to take your fellow man's one away. I don't remember exactly what I said that day, but all in all, it was that to me it was understandable that men who know nothing about religion would turn themselves into beasts, however it was totally incomprehensible that religious men allowed and even blessed those who give themselves to such barbarity.

I never forgot this scene. I came out of combat without a scratch, but deeply moved after seeing dying, almost defenseless, so many youngsters. The chaplain, who had assisted helping the injured under the enemy's fire, sat down next to me on a tree trunk, put an arm over my shoulders when I broke down into tears and said to me that he understood how I felt. For an instant I thought I was crying from repentance, but I soon realized that it was the nervous tension from the combat that made me weaken. However, in my consciousness remained the feeling of having committed a sacrilege by saying what I had said about God.

Therefore, I considered myself unworthy of receiving the holy sacraments. And honestly saying, I was also afraid of the penance resulting from confessing such a thing.

For this reason, and perhaps also because I wanted to expiate, in my own way, my sin, without it being too uncomfortable, I went to that temple only in the afternoons when it was more or less empty.

Due to the war I had lost, naturally, all faith in miracles. On the other hand, the international news, which I had to translate daily, indicated to me that miracles belonged to times already too remote to be taken into account. It is true that once in a while some paragraph arrived announcing some miraculous cure in Lourdes. But the miracle I expected was very far from happening, as I was hoping for the miracle of peace.

What happened to me in my own country was happening to the Ethiopians and Italians in Africa. Soon after, in the name of supposedly noble principles and with the participation of the religion and the religious, it started to happen in Spain. In such a way that back then I knew in my heart that there was no miracle for me, unless from my part I did what I needed to do and at my own risk.

However, I couldn't hide inside me that profound faith in Jesus Christ. Even when I had blasphemed saying that I considered God rubbish, reason indicated to me that if I took literally the principle that He was in heaven, on earth and everywhere, I couldn't lose anything by making Him see or explaining to Him that crisis suffered in the war. I also thought that with time it could be possible to persuade Him to help me earn enough money to treat my leg and be able to work normally. So then, when I arrived at the church I prayed in a hurry one Our Father, one Hail Mary and one My Lord Jesus Christ. Immediately after, I address myself to that beautiful image of the Heart of Jesus, telling Him:

"My Lord, Jesus Christ, what I ask you for is not much. I know you can't give me the lottery, and even if it was possible for you to do it, I'm not so much interested in money. I'm neither going to ask you to help me find an heiress. For the moment I don't want to get married. Besides, what heiress would want to marry me when she finds out that I only want her so she can pay my leg operation? Only a very ugly woman would do it, and I don't want to get married with an ugly woman. I don't want to get married to a very beautiful one either because, if she is rich as well as pretty, with certainty she will be stupid and shallow. Do you know what my grandfather used to say? He said: 'give me the death of a wise man, but not the life of a dumb one.' You well know that I have it in my blood. That's why, my Lord Jesus Christ, the only thing I ask of you is for something that others seem to underestimate as useless and superfluous: I ask you for intelligence. Only help me to have more intelligence, and from then onwards I will manage on my own and I will not bother you anymore."

One of my counted qualities is perseverance when something interests me vitally. What I wanted back then was to open a way and become a great foreign correspondent. For that purpose, in my bed-sit at night, I would rehearse the most sensationalists' articles that I could imagine based on what I was learning with my job. I used to create a series of political events of which I was a privileged witness. I very well knew that these were crazy dreams but I enjoyed dreaming them. It was also marvelous to observe that somewhere inside me there was someone capable of dreaming. Little by little, taking as a base the experience that my job gave me, I started to write articles about the international situation. I enjoyed a lot doing predictions on what was going to happen as a consequence of a given fact. These predictions were based on certain phenomenon, which I noticed kept repeating over and over again, virtually in every great event. They seemed to obey a principle, and this principle governed the actions of great men. This made me resume the study of history, which had specially attracted me at school. I started to understand it from another point of view, noticing at the same time that this repetition happened automatically from the most remote of times. Everything came down to understanding the motives; the motives were always the same ones and gave life to everything. In such a way that when my predictions started to fulfill with more or less precision, I decided to intensify my requests to Jesus Christ. I made them more serious and of more scope. I noted my predictions down in a little notebook and after a few months I started to complete my work very efficiently and much faster, which caused a slight increase in my salary. I was also earning a few extra dollars making messages signed under an assumed name, classifying them as great internationalists and dating them in any European capital. The newspapers that were buying this material had a soft spot for Anglo-Saxon names.

I felt then obliged to show my gratitude in some way and decided to go to the temple earlier and stay longer. I started my petitions very meticulously:

"My Lord Jesus Christ: thank you for listening to me. Every time I see it more clearly. They have increased my salary, but the operation costs a lot more. So then I ask you to give me more intelligence and I won't continue bothering you like this."

I also detailed to Him my personal problems and asked Him for advice saying:

"Enlighten me so that I can understand more clearly."

This gathering at the temple turned into a beneficial habit and, of course, economical, as while my friends played dice in pubs or went to the cinema for entertainment, I went to pray. And the money that I would have spent with them was turning into an increasing amount, which I was depositing into a savings account.

I waited patiently for the day that I could leave the limp, the stick and the crutch and throw myself into the adventure of dropping the translations to get into the career of journalist of sensationalist matters.

3

At that time I met my friend. Like me, this man of a seemingly concentrated appearance, always occupied the same place in the temple. He prayed with great devotion. I felt attracted to that particular way of praying. He didn't move his lips, his face didn't shine a grave expression but it was all serenity. He prayed with his arms as a cross and didn't take his eyes away from the image of Jesus Christ. Often because of looking at him, I got distracted from my own prayers. I thought that perhaps it was good to have that power of concentration and be able to address Our Lord Jesus Christ as is right and proper. But even when I perceived such wishes within me, the idea of imitating him displeased me. My grandfather always had said to me that we pray with the heart and not with the mind. I never worried to go deep into these things, and because of reasons that were born as a result of my education, I refused decisively to recite the classic prayers unless they were those that moved me. At school I had received many and very painful wallopings because of my impertinence about the real sense and practicality of prayers. But there was no walloping strong enough to defeat my stubbornness and, my teachers managed with them to turn me into an obstinate rebel.

This man seemed to measure with precision the duration of his prayers. He always arrived before me. I never saw him coming in after me, but he finished one or two minutes after me. He crossed himself in a very solemn way, however without the slight affectation. I noticed that he stopped his hand in the established points for longer time that the priests themselves. One afternoon I thought that maybe to cross one self in that way had a very special meaning. This man didn't wet his fingers in the holy water stoup either. He left very silently. After some days, observing that I watched his doings, he commenced to greet me with a slight nod. It was then when I noticed that there was something out of the ordinary in his appearance. His expression was of goodness, but also indicated a great strength. And when I moved away from the temple to go to work, I saw him in the stairs either lighting or smoking a cigarette.

One afternoon when there was plenty of news and more critical than usual, I went out of the temple together with him as I was in a hurry to get to my work. As we reached the door we bumped into each other. My limp was an obstacle and, wanting to let him go first, I moved suddenly and dropped my stick on the floor. Instead of going out, he bent down immediately and handed it to me saying:

"I apologize; it was clumsiness on my behalf."

I was astonished as there was no doubt that the clumsy was me as I had the childish urge to take the lead, and only when I realized that I could cause him to stumble, I let it drop.

I should say that I was quite used to people's reprimands because of my clumsiness, especially in the trams. In one occasion, in the same church, a very devoted lady had reprimanded me when she tripped over the walking stick that I had carelessly left by my side. And when I apologized for my negligence, she said to me:

"For something God punished you in that way, inconsiderate!"

I didn't doubt for an instance that this lady was right as I had sinned so seriously in the war, so then I assumed that her words were a warning to be more careful with the stick that caused trouble to such devoted lady. I also thought that the advice included a warning to never come to the temple with crutches. The lady had rushed to get to the confessional box where there was a long queue of dames waiting their turn. When I looked at that one who I troubled so much, I realized that I was also to blame for the fact that I had made her lose two spaces in the queue, due to the time she had to employ to remind me of my sins and blasphemies. She was turning her rosary with agitated and nervous hands, and I gathered that this lady really needed to confess in a hurry.

I tell this incident because it had already encrusted within me a certain resignation to receive imprecations from good people whom my stick and my limp bothered so much. Because of this, when this strange man apologized for something for which I was the only one to blame, I couldn't bring myself to say anything. I was so surprised before such novelty. I remembered trying to say something but I don't know if I could articulate a word. He opened the thin door very carefully, stepped to the side and invited me:

"Please go first; surely, you are in a hurry."

I only managed to nod my head in a sign of gratitude. Only outside I could recover from the amazement and said:

"You know well that it was my fault. You are very kind. Thank you very much."

It's necessary here to point out something very singular that I felt in that moment. The deference that he demonstrated produced in me a very curious irritation. I waited for him to respond with the anticipated: "by no means." I waited wishing he would say it because he would have disappointed me if he had. What was the reason for me to have such a strange wish?

I still can't explain it.

But he didn't say it and then something unusual happened. I felt a lively happiness from his brief and silent bow. And I said to myself:

"Thank goodness this one is not a slob."

After his assent, he went away. I started to step down the temple with the typical lumpishness of the lame only being able to come down one step at a time. And that day the descent was awfully slow for me. I felt behind me that he was observing and sympathizing with me. Usually, the compassion that some expressed with my lameness had a flavour of hypocrisy and irritated me a lot. I classified it false mercy, a form of trivia like any other.

Once more I had to change my way of thinking about this man. My judgement had been very impulsive. When I reached the footpath, I looked back and saw him walking away in the opposite direction as if nothing had happened.

I didn't remember this incident until the next day when I came into the temple. Because of certain arrangements that were getting done in the interior, the benches that he and I used to pray on weren't in the usual position. This man had occupied the end of the only bench from which the altar could be seen. And that end was touching a thick pillar. I accommodated myself in the same bench but a bit far away from him and had the cautiousness of placing the stick behind me, on the seat. When he had finished his prayers, he sat down; I didn't realize this fact until I had finished myself and was getting ready to leave. The man had waited patiently, as to come out he would have had to interrupt me. Such fineness moved me, so much more as I had perceived his custom of abandoning the temple as soon as he finished his prayers. I looked at him, smiled and said:

"Thank you very much, sir."

He did once again a bow with the head, stood up and waited for me to accommodate the posture of my leg and to pick up my stick. I tried to do it as fast as possible to return his fineness, and due to a rough move, I felt such a sharp pain that, without realising I was doing it, I exclaimed:

"Shit!"

I already had the stick in my right hand. I let it drop to hold the back of the seat, and with my left hand I could touch the painful part of my leg. When I bent I realized what I just said, feeling my face alight from embarrassment. But he smiled immutable, and with the same expression kind and amiable, said as if it was the most natural thing:

"Amen."

So violent was the shock that produced in me, that I couldn't hold my laugh and it was necessary to cover my mouth to avoid provoking a scandal. I just said a barbarity in front of this man who, obviously, took very seriously this religious function. However, not only didn't he demonstrate violence or annoyance, but he had even dissipated my embarrassment and my guiltiness in such way that I had fallen into the most open hilarity. Because even if I'm violent, I have an easy laugh. One thing goes with the other.

I made an effort and collected myself as best I could. I took the stick and started to come out with my usual clumsiness. That man didn't even make a gesture to help me, and because of it I felt grateful. His 'amen' was already a remarkable concession of my weakness.

When we were outside, however, I felt obliged to give an explanation, so I stopped him and said:

"I beg you pardon, Sir. Believe me, it was an involuntary exclamation. The pain was very sharp."

"I understand," he said to me. "Those pains are certainly sharp. Due to the circumstances, your exclamation was natural.

No need to apologize to me."

I confess that a long time passed before I understood his response. Even now it seems inexplicable. But at that time I didn't think about it, as I was more preoccupied in formulating my apologies and to correspond with respect to the condescension he had with me, so I said to him:

"I realize that my exclamation has probably hurt your devotion. You have been too deferent with me and I wouldn't want to cause you displeasure. After all, my devotion is not the same as yours; I don't come to the temple to adore nor to apologize for my sins because I know they don't have forgiveness and, also I don't deserve it. I come to ask for help on necessities not very spiritual. As you can see, I sum one sin to another, and all because of a pain in the leg."

It was in this opportunity when he directed his first paradox. Talking very intentionally and slowly, he said:

"Same as good and virtue, sin and evil can only be given in vigil. Who sleeps, sleeps; for the asleep there is no sin, as there is no good, nor virtue. There is only sleep."

I looked at him expressing certain suspicion of finding myself in front of a crazy man, however his look was so clean, it was fixed in my eyes, without being impertinent, that I hesitated before completing my judgement. I didn't say anything. He continued:

"In reality, no one sins deliberately; no one can do evil deliberately. In sleep things are the way they are and they are the only way they can be. When one is asleep, one doesn't have control nor dominance over what happens in dreams."

"I confess I can't understand you," I said.

"It's only natural that is so. Forget this incident that doesn't have any major importance."

"But I'm afraid that I hurt you with that completely involuntary expression."

"No, you didn't hurt me in any way. You have hurt yourself. The great majority of men hurt themselves in that way, precisely because everything they think, feel and do is involuntary."

"I would like to understand you. What you are telling me is very confusing and I lament that my worries don't allow me to reflect upon the meaning of your words."

"Even in sleep man has a certain power of election, very limited by the way; but he has. In any way, when he puts it into practice, this power increases. If his interest in understanding is sincere and deep, he won't find it difficult to realize that the man who is asleep can choose between waking up or to keep sleeping."

I wasn't interested in riddles of this kind. However, I was attracted to the way he talked. But I was in a hurry to get to my office to see if my last forecast had come through or not. Besides, the general crisis in Europe had everyone very busy, so my spirit wasn't predisposed to meditate upon the things it just heard. To avoid being rude, I said to him:

"Surely what you say is very true. At least, in my case it is. I feel releaved for not having offended your religious feelings. I will try to be more careful in the future. Now, please excuse me as I have to go to my work."

I was about to tell him the usual 'see you later,' when he interrupted me:

"I don't have a fixed direction, so if you allow me, I will accompany you."

I had always avoided the company of friends and acquaintances, knowing that my lameness made them impatient, as I had to drag my injured leg. I was about to say no, that I was in a hurry, when I noticed the incongruity of my excuse. I couldn't, in any way, talk about walking fast. Not knowing what to do, I just said:

"With great pleasure."

But inside I was boiling with fury. This man was imposing over my will in a very soft way, at the same time so resolved, that I couldn't hide my irritation and started to move in silence. Each of his gestures was, however, considered. While I was descending with difficulty the steps of the temple towards the footpath, he told me that he was going to go ahead of me to buy cigarettes. When we were together again, he played with the packet and when we reached the corner he didn't have that pitiful gesture, which irritated me so much from everyone, of helping me to cross to the other side. He walked beside me very naturally, as if my walking was that of a normal man. Nevertheless, he seemed to intercept my internal irritation, as he said to me:

"The pains that you suffer were as you expressed them in the church. I would like you to pull them out of yourself."

This only increased my irritation. I was about to tell him that compassion was sickening and that, in any way, what would he care whether I was or not suffering pain. But something stopped me and I remained in silence. I started to remember that I also had, more than once, wished vividly the disappearance of the pains that others more seriously injured suffered, especially in hospitals of blood. So I thought that maybe this man wasn't a hypocrite telling me what he thought about mine. I started to feel more relaxed and at the same time gained more confidence towards him. He offered me a cigarette and, observing my gesture to look for matches with the stick hanging from my arm, he let me do it. I felt sympathy for him, and decided to confide my shameful secret:

"I hope not to offend you with what I'm about to tell you, but in reality I go to church to see if with the prayers I get a bit more understanding to better carry out my occupation. I hope like this to get a pay rise. I need it and I work extra hours to be able to afford my leg operation and be cured. But don't think that I hope for a miracle; I also ask for other things that might be too stingy."

"I understand," he said to me.

"I hope to get together the necessary sum very soon. When I can walk well, I will be able to work better and make a career and a name."

"Apparently, you have a very precise purpose."

"Well, without a precise purpose there is very little that one can do," I said.

"It is a great thing to have a precise purpose, to know what one wants. It is much more important than many imagine. But counted are the men that really know what they want in life; some believe to know, but they are mistaken. They confuse the goals with the means they use, and it sometimes happens that the means are their real goal. But since they see them as means, because they can't see further or better, they use great and sublime means for pretty stingy objectives. Like this is how knowledge gets prostituted."

This comment gave me a bad feeling inside and I answered:

"Are you referring to my case, to the fact that I don't go to church with spiritual goals?"

"No," he said to me. "I talk in general terms. I don't think you have authorized me to treat directly intimate things of yours. Aside from this, when I want to say something I say it directly and without evasion."

"Maybe my attitude at church sparks your attention. But the case is that I don't know how to pray neither I know how to adore. I only know how to ask, and I ask in my own way. Religion stopped interesting me for many reasons."

"But, apparently, you haven't lost your faith and that is what really matters; more so in your particular case. There is a lot to say about faith. It is something that must grow in man.

And in regards to knowing how to pray, it is simpler than what you suppose. In our times the meaning of the prayer has become very complex. My opinion is that when it is known what one wants and one fights to achieve it, even if it is not formulated in words, one is in a permanent prayer. Sometime I read somewhere that all profound wanting is a prayer and that never remains without response; man always receives what he asks for. But, since man generally doesn't know what his heart really wants, neither he knows how to ask for what is convenient for him. From this I consider the Lord's Prayer, for example, an accessible prayer only to the heart thirsty of truth and hungry of goodness. All true miracles depend on this, but the modern man doesn't see it this way any more, and has also lost the true meaning of the miraculous. He looks for it outside of himself, in the phenomenal. The modern man has forgotten many simple things and this forgetfulness is the underlying truth in the concept of the original sin."

"I don't believe in miracles," I responded.

"It is possible that your formulation is so. But allow me to put in doubt your words."

"How am I not going to know what I believe myself?"

"Facts reveal it. It is very simple, if you observe them well. If you wouldn't believe in miracles, you wouldn't go to the church."

I have enjoyed very much your company. I am grateful. Maybe we can come back to these issues if you are interested in them. Are you going to the church tomorrow?

"Surely," I said. "If I'm alive."

"And if God allows it," he added very seriously.

I remained confused. This last expression had annoyed me. For moments this man seemed judiciousness itself, but his paradoxes and contradictions mortified me. In any way, I said to myself, at least he is honest and he is not a slob.

4

We walked together again the next day. And also the day after. And like this, we consolidated a beautiful and sincere friendship. His paradoxes hit me only from time to time. He made sure that I was eating well and that I was enjoying enough rest. He persuaded me to the point of making me abandon the extra work that was depriving me from sleep and rest. He helped me to do forecasts and soon I had several books full of notes. But the most concerning thing for him seemed to be my leg. And one day, very timidly, he adventured to tell me:

"I have discussed your case with a surgeon friend of mine. If you can pay the x-rays, he will operate on you for free. You will be able to pay the expenses of hospital, anaesthetics, war, etc., monthly. Are you interested?"

"Of course!" I exclaimed. "I was full of joy."

At this stage we had become closer and knew each other better. His frank and open way to do things attracted me; especially the way he threw his opinions without worrying about mine. But he had dropped the religious aspect, which didn't stop surprising me.

I got permission from my bosses to be absent from the office, they even gave me a pay in advance so I could complete my payments. That memorable afternoon, my friend waited for me at the church door.

"We are late," he told me. "Let's catch a taxi."

During the trip he didn't talk and neither did I, except:

"It is a shame that I couldn't pray this afternoon. I would have liked to say thank you for all this."

"Be calm in this regard," he answered. "It has been given, received and you are at peace with Him."

I didn't even have time to get surprised because in that instance we arrived at the clinic and he anticipated paying the driver.

Those five weeks went so fast that I almost can't remember the details. He visited me every day; he took care of certain personal matters that I couldn't understand, and when the doctor gave me the authorization to get up and to try to walk, he went away.

My first days without walking stick, still in the clinic, were pretty unpleasant. I had developed the habit of limping and missed the walking stick. My friend told me:

"Every habit is an acquired thing and one can change it. Try this test."

And putting a box of matches in my hand, he indicated:

"Press it in your hand as if it were the handle of the walking stick."

After a few tries I started to realize that doing it this way I felt more secure and walked better. Time went by and I was discharged as being cured. That day my friend came to get me and we left the clinic together. When I thanked the surgeon for his kindness for not charging me for the operation, I noticed he got confused. Much later I knew that this confusion was due to the fact that my friend had paid for all the expenses. He never gave me the opportunity to be grateful for this gesture.

When we left the clinic and I was walking beside him happily, he made a few paradoxical comments:

"People think that habits are left behind when in reality one can only change them. The wisdom of man is proven justly in which habits he changes and which he adopts in place of the ones he thinks he leaves behind. I say this to you with a double purpose: The main one is that you start to get to know yourself; the other one, to indicate a detail for which you can get the run of this knowledge that some very wise man consider indispensable for human happiness. For example, now you are pressing the matchbox, hiding this habit by having the hand in your pocket. This is not necessarily harmful. I say it only so you can learn to self observe. For now it is enough that you know it. You could have continued to believe that you had left behind the habit of the stick, but what you have left behind is only the walking stick and not the habit of leaning on something to walk. Now you lean on a box of matches. I don't know if you understand what I want to say."

I pulled my hand out of my pocket immediately, somehow ashamed, but he said:

"No, that wasn't my intention. You haven't understood me. See you could have changed the habit of walking leaning on something for the habit of reacting with an exaggerated pride and that would have been really harmful. Wisdom is to have insight into these things, into these subtleties, because of these subtleties is made everything that is big. When we want to be better and don't necessary know for ourselves what is best or what is worse, we easily fall in absurdities and become slaves to what others determine best or worse. In every human being there is a Judge always ready to guide us; but due to our bad education and the consequences of this and other things, either we ignore this Internal Judge or, when he talks to us, we don't pay the due attention. This Judge is ourselves in a different form, let's say invisible. I would dare to say that in your case it was this Judge who made you go to the church and who has guided you in many of your tribulations. To remember this Judge, to practice its presence in oneself, is a very important thing. And since it is, let's say, a superior aspect of ourselves, we can call this Judge *I*. But not that ordinary *I* we know. Striving to feel him in each of our actions, of our feelings, of our thoughts, nourish him. Eventually we can get to notice him as something highly extraordinary, highly intelligent and understanding. It is a very different sensation and feeling to what we are used to considering as *I*. It doesn't appear overnight, but it needs to be forged patiently. But it is enough for now. Think about this, I beg you. Do you like cycling?"

I answered yes.

"Magnificent," he said. "If you want, when I come back from a trip I must make now, we can start a series of rides together. Fortunately I have two; one is from a brother who died. Would you like these outings?"

"Of course I would," I said.

In reality, free from my lameness, I felt that the world was a marvellous thing. I said good-bye to my friend. The next day I went to the church much sooner than usual. I expressed my gratitude to Jesus and when I was whispering my improvised speech, I remember the words of my friend in his first talk:

"If you wouldn't believe in the miraculous, you wouldn't go to church."

I realized that in everything that I had just lived, a miracle had happened, but I wasn't entirely convinced. Everything had happened too casually, and also I was used to thinking that miracles, for them to be real, had to happen in a few seconds. Mine was delayed almost one year and this wasn't for me a miracle. Maybe whoever is reading this can explain the reason why there was a voice, an idea, something in me that insisted that a miracle had happened, but I didn't manage to find one that completely satisfied me, even though my friend talked often about *the illusion of time*. In what he asked me to publish there is mention of time and of love, which I frankly don't understand. I have limited myself to type up the notebooks that he gave me.

But let's come back to him.

5

As I said earlier, I never knew his name, his real name. Sometimes he said that names lack importance, what is really important is closer to us than our own name, which is more real than our name. He said that names are only a social convenience, a way of identifying ourselves. Sometimes he said that he felt identified with certain strange bees of Yucatan, sometimes with Prince Canek, who had been loved by Princess Sac-Nicté; other times he used to say that his love for the sun urged him to feel of the same spirit as a certain Inca called Yahuar Huakak whose inquietudes he shared for a time even though there were a large amount of centuries between them. Other times he shared with me that he was in love with the wisdom of the Ioanes and with some of the things of Melchisedec.

Very often I heard him comment:

"The only thing that really matters is *to be*. Man *is*, the rest that he has is by addition."

Amongst my notes back then, I found registered some of his words: "Time, the development of life and the occurrences of man are something that few take into account and that an even a smaller number are capable of understanding. Life is a miracle in itself, but we rarely pertain to consider. We take for granted many things that are not true, that will stop being true if we would apply to them a question, a why? We don't know who we really are, or what it is that we really are, what desires are the ones that really move us. Few are the ones that are convinced of this. The majority thinks that with a name, a profession and other circumstantial things, they know everything. Our way of thinking is still very naive. Much of which man attributes to modern education has to be searched for in the depths of the purest psychology, which is something that has been lost. But also there are many psychologists who don't even understand the things they say. Otherwise they would have already discarded the psychoanalysis. Ordinary science doesn't believe nor accepts the miraculous because it is not truly scientific. There are men of science who occasionally and for moral reasons, talk about the spiritual, but they don't even stop to consider what is matter in itself. There are men apparently spiritual who don't realize the transcendental meaning of what Jesus said to Nicodemus, which is registered in the gospel with these words: *'If I have told you earthly things, and ye believe not, how shall ye believe if I tell you of heavenly things?'* And the thing is that science doesn't want to notice that in the words, the parables, the miracles and all known facts of Jesus, there is a lot more science that we could ordinarily imagine. Due to this, the philosophy that we know is based on anti-scientific ingenuousness, in the same way that the Christian religion is at odds with the principal truths that Christ taught. But we cannot despair. There are those who know the key of true science and their knowledge is exact and precise, and one can't go wrong about them. The only difficulty is that to this science and to this knowledge no one arrives by chance. One needs to search for them with eagerness and prepare oneself for a long time. But we can all get in contact with these men, we can make contact through their ideas and, above all, through the efforts we make in understanding them. It is the sincere effort that has worth. There is a lot of this, especially in literature. Few suspect that a small book that costs a few cents could contain the most marvellous teachings that one could desire. Like I say, we think very naive; better said, we don't know how to think. For example, science and philosophy use methods that, if they would examine, they would turn them into goals. One of these methods is known with the name *intuition*. Science ignores how much it owes to intuition; the same thing happens with philosophy. It is about a recording or speed different to the function of human intelligence. We can say the same about art and religion. The revelations in which the religious dogma is based, are something that all theologians want to elaborate about without realising that at the speed at which the ordinary reason works, it is material impossible of elaboration."

"What book is the one that costs a few cents?," I asked.

'The sermon of the Mountain. It is the sum of chapters five, six and seven of the Gospel of Saint Mathew."

"Why doesn't religion say anything about this?"

My friend looked at me and smiled.

"Religion doesn't realize that its error relies exactly in the concept that it has of *religion*. However, to be able to understand the truth of this concept it is necessary to disregard the ordinary concept."

I was astonished before such gibberish.

"But you are obviously a religious man. How can you say that?"

"You see it," he answered. "You can't come out of the coffin in which your education has enclosed you, your concept of religious morals, etc. Many men often notice the possibility of coming out of the coffin, and understand the word coffin literally; they stick their heads to the borders, but the idea of freedom that they see scares them and they soon come back to their coffins and even close the top with spikes so nothing disturbs their sleep."

"But why do you say to me that religion is a mistaken concept?"

"Religion means re-link and there is nothing to be re-linked because there is nothing in the Universe that is unlinked from anything. However, we need to represent things as they were unlinked due to the limitations of our senses and to the understanding derived from that limitation. How could the concept of re-link be compatible with the most elemental thing of the catechism, for example, that God is in heaven, earth and everywhere? Or that other affirmation of one of the fathers of the church, Paul the Apostle, who said: *'In God we live, we move and we have our being.'*"

"So then, what must we do?"

"Be aware of the meaning of the word *Universe*; struggle to raise intelligence to those states of sharpness where these ideas are alive. Once again we can return to the encounter of Nicodemus with Jesus, because on the same regard Jesus gave the key of understanding of these things when he said: *'And no man hath ascended up to heaven, but he that came down from heaven, even the Son of man which is in heaven. And as Moses lifted up the serpent in the wilderness, even so must the Son of man be lifted up: That whosoever believeth in him should not perish, but have eternal life.'*"

"This is extremely difficult to understand."

"It all depends on the effort you make to understand. The effort to understand these affirmations which seem so obscure is precisely the key that can open the doors of heaven for us; but the majority goes along with the first interpretation they find, forgetting the effort and like this they start to fall, the original sin starts. Because it means to stop the development of intelligence. When this development is stopped, when man is satisfied with the comprehension of today and doesn't try to extend it to the maximum intensity that he is capable of, he loses his capacity, he loses his comprehension and eventually loses his soul; better said, mutilates, obstructs his growth in such way that the soul gets sick and can even die completely. This is something Jesus tried to explain in the parable of the talents, of the wedding dress and, above all, in those two words that one finds in every instant in the Gospels: *'Watch and pray.'*

With time I got used to this so special language of my friend. I introduced him to some of my companions, and when they asked me who he was, I didn't know what to respond, so I decided to tell them that he was a relative of mine, a bit eccentric, but a good person deep inside.

When I informed him of this with the hidden hope that he would tell me the truth about himself, he commented:

"Our true relationship is much more real that what you imagine. You will find out about it sometime."

"Don't you think you are exaggerating a bit this mystery?" I said.

"The truth always seems an exaggeration to those who don't observe it."

"It is a bit difficult to take."

"I don't doubt it. But you don't realize that we speak different languages, because we have a different understanding."

"So then, why don't we talk mine?"

"Because even though you are not well aware of it, you want to learn mine. If I would have guided myself through your words, we would have stopped seeing each other and talking long ago. I don't speak with what you appear to be through your words, but with what you could be."

"This is real gibberish. Is this all you have to say to me?"

"What I say to you will always depend on what you want to ask me."

Even though these interviews always left me uneasy, to notice how he always managed my thoughts and deflected my intentions, I couldn't help my fondness for him increasing. It was something very contradictory that was happening inside of me.

Time went by. I continued holding the box of matches that I carried always in my pocket, and I couldn't forget the war. Most of all, I couldn't forget the feeling of repugnance towards myself every time the memory came back to me of a certain man who died after I stuck a bayonet in his abdomen. His agony was so horrible to see that for instances I wished the dead man to be me. This scene came back to me more frequently now that the war offices were giving the number of casualties on the different fronts. I couldn't take these figures as if they were just figures; for me they represented human suffering which affected not only the troops, but each soldier and each man was the centre of a tragedy for a whole family, for a whole circle of friends and maybe for the earth itself. I couldn't explain where and how these thoughts came to me, but I felt an internal uneasiness that sometimes turned into something painful. So I did everything possible to run away from those moments and even got to feel envy for the coldness with which my colleagues shuffled these figures. It also amazed me each time I saw the heading of the newspapers registering them as though they were events without importance in the history of the world, and like truly glorious actions. The press paid lots of money to have this news; in the same way, people pleasantly paid money to read it.

The war had turned into a ghost that hounded my conscience. Of ten messages that were reaching my hands to be edited, nine were directly about the war and the tenth indirectly. Like this time past in Ethiopia, Spain and one day it reached Poland and finally the war extended throughout the world. This fact was so overwhelming that by the force of their numbers, the messages started to cloud me. Little by little I became harder with so much replication of figures about dead, injured and missing people. One day I noticed that I was interested and that I was enjoying the description of the bombing of a city where thousands and thousands of women, children and old people had died, all of them completely defenceless before the rain of fire that was landing over them. By coincidence, that same day I had translated a message that contained certain declarations made by an important chief of the International Red Cross. It was about the five points in regards to the help and protection of children and I had decided to keep a copy for me. I left it at my working desk and when I wanted to take it, the other messages about dead, injured, bombings and naval encounters had covered it completely. I thought for an instant about this apparently accidental fact and realized that the same thing that happened to the Red Cross message was happening to my own feelings. And in that moment I remembered the imploring eyes of that boy who I had injured with the bayonet and thought to see in them a reproach that was saying to me: "So soon you have forgotten?"

Each war message repeated this scene in my memory and together with it thoughts of hope crossed me; I wanted to believe that the soul of this boy had reached some compensation in another life.

A very subtle and very powerful fear began to overtake me when I realized that I was also becoming hard. My colleagues joked with me about these scruples and even some argued that wars, specially a this big war, will bring a great scientific progress so luckily we could raise hopes for a better life and world. The incongruity of this argument ended up disgusting me. History was the best witness that wars only produced new and bloodier wars. There were these messages indicating to me how the history of this period was going to be written. Comparing them with those of last war, human cruelty had increased, hatred had intensified. Can we expect a better world based on greater cruelty? Or a better life based on a more intense hatred that was eating everything under the legend of *total war*? In those days, I remembered a phrase from Lincoln: 'Human progress is within the human heart.' And wasn't I witnessing that my own heart was in love with that cruelty and hatred?

This singular fear, a cold fear, as if death was threatening in each thought, increased rapidly. When I encountered my friend again I told him this and many other reflections that I had made.

"Yes," he said. "It is natural. The soul always knows what it wants, and when it starts to awaken, it commences to ask its own things. There is something in all men that refuses to get tricked by the first explanation that reaches the senses. Some pay attention to this silent voice, others don't. It is very painful and unpleasant at the beginning. It is the first threshold. When in a man there is a commencement of genuine life, the power of all that leads him to sleep is also fortified. This is a dangerous period of time because all awakening gives new energies. And everything that is false within our personality takes advantage of them and our slavery increases. It can be said without mistake much that like this the soul gets killed. Like this we have in the world many souls whose life has stopped and little by little start losing the possibility of growth and perfection, which is a right that man doesn't use. There are souls that are decidedly dead. The human being is more than body and senses, but he doesn't know, he doesn't understand."

"Are you telling me that the soul is not immortal?," I asked.

"That depends on the person," he told me.

"But that is where the religious principles are, Plato's writings and the affirmations of many men recognized as intelligent who assure that we have an immortal soul."

"You sleep still."

"Are you going to contradict Plato?"

"I could clarify many points so you can understand Plato, but you are not ready yet."

"I don't understand you."

"You are blinded by your own ideas, and as long as you stay in such a condition you cannot understand anything. Observe a fact: if the soul was something that we have naturally secured, religious writings wouldn't insist so much that we need to make an effort to save it. There wouldn't be a need for philosophy or religion. We would know it naturally and no one would fear death as they do. Listen to me: we form the soul in this life based on what animates us. If the motives, ideals and ambitions of our life are transitory, they are things of the immediate moment then our soul will also be transitory, impermanent, subject to what we want. One day you will be able to reflect calmly upon these things and you will understand that boy whose death obsesses you. Observe well: you didn't kill him from yourself because from yourself you can't do anything. So something that it is not yourself, a society, trained you, taught you to kill. Remember that exclamation of yours inside the church? Well, it is the same. Your exclamation and the bayonet thrust were involuntary. If before throwing that exclamation you would have been able to realize the fact, you would not have said it; the same thing with the bayonet thrust. A bit of reflection and you would not have done it. But in those moments there is no time for reflection. Listen well to what I say: there is no time. So then to be able to act with the heart, it is necessary to overcome time and this demands a kind of will that you don't know yet. To achieve this will requires great efforts, great obedience and something superior. Have you observed and considered about philanthropy, charity? A man who for years had been subject to the type of training I'm talking about couldn't avoid doing good deeds; to do it would be a function almost instinctive in him. He will do it naturally. But the majority of people think that just by doing good deeds they will achieve something, which can only be achieved intentionally, going against stream within oneself. In regards to the immortality of the soul, there is no doubt that it exists; but saying that it is immortal, it is another story. Try to understand that I'm talking about the individual man."

"My God! Now I really think you are crazy! ," I exclaimed.

"As you wish," he said smiling.

"Are you trying to tell me that we are all wrong?"

"Why not?"

"It is not possible."

"You are very naive. You have a living example within yourself and even then you argue with vehemence. But it doesn't matter. Do you see what a mistake it would be if I would guide myself only by your words? You know and feel that the war is horrible, that it is something barbarian, the culmination of all savagery within man. You know that your colleagues are wrong about those numbers of casualties; however, for you each number is the representation of a human being and that makes you suffer. Those who don't feel what they think will be always wrong. Observe that all this horror is happening in what we call the Christian world, and one of the main precepts of Christian culture says: You shall not kill! But man starts to kill in the heart before killing of action; the death that you see around you commenced with hatred. And society justifies it in many ways to shout down the voice of the conscience, if they ever pay attention to it. Which of the Christian churches has adopted a vigorous, unambiguous attitude towards this war? Only a few isolated men have opposed it and have preferred to sacrifice their lives in laboratory experiments. Let's go back to the interview of old Nicodemus with Jesus. This interview happened in times as agitated as now, when a form of culture was falling down while another one was brewing. And Jesus said to Nicodemus that it was necessary to be born again, to be born of water and spirit, to be able to enjoy the attributes that correspond to a true soul."

"But many who die, die convinced that their soul is going to survive."

"I don't doubt it. The human being is convinced of many things. There was a time when he was convinced that the world was flat. If you examine the Gospels, you will see that they say clearly: *'What will it be worth for you to win the world if you are going to lose the soul?'*

I found it impossible to argue with him. My interest for the Holy Scriptures was minimal. I had not read them or studied them. However, something was telling me intimately that my friend was right even if I understood nothing. After a short silence, I told him:

"Isn't it then enough to obey what religion says?"

"To obey faithfully and from the heart the ordinary precepts of religion is the first step, an indispensable step. Everything is interlaced, everything is united. Religious forms are the external appearance of what can be called the internal church. And this one is truly immortal. To that is the Credo referring when it talks about The Communion of the Saints."

So then I took the advantage to ask him to explain to me the true way to pray.

"You have been praying intensely, but without noticing."

I answered by telling him my experiences as a student.

"You see," he told me, "ignorance was about to blind you completely. And now you are the one that denies the food that your soul needs. Don't think that you can now blame your teachers, your confessors or your parents. You could have done it until not long ago; but now that is forbidden to you. If you want to know more about the Lord's Prayer, for example, start to puzzle out what to forgive those who trespass against us really means. I tell you these things because sincere ignorance is forgivable, but not hypocrisy, lies, nor laziness."

"And how can I do this?"

"In the same way you have done the rest. For example, that verse that says *'deliver us from all evil'* you have lived it in your own way. And to live a plea is more important than to formulate it. You went to the church to ask for more intelligence, as you have told me. Intelligence is exactly an attribute of the kingdom of heaven. You were given understanding. The other verse: *'lead us not into temptation'* you have experienced it in the horror you lived because of the fact that you were turning hard inside."

"But this is a very strange way of praying." I told him shocked.

"It is the only way of the heart. To understand prayers it is necessary to have an idea, at least a close one of the Communion of the Saints. Each of the prayers that we know is a synthetised treatise of knowledge of great scope. It is psychology that ordinary psychologist ignore. The Lord's Prayer, for example, can be for an individual the Jacob's ladder to reach heaven, if the individual lives it. For a physician it can be the way to explain the nature of the Universe. And I know a man dedicated to astronomy that has understood it for the benefit of his studies. These prayers are the work of the Communion of the Saints. Now, the Communion of the Saints has a lot of names, depending on the creed that each race practices. It is not an established organisation, but a beat of universal life. They are the guardians of culture and of civilization, God's Helpers."

"Often you speak about the food of the soul. What are you referring to?"

"To a type of food as real as the one the body needs. This follows from the words of Jesus: *'Man does not live on bread alone, but of every word of God.'* The physical food contains energies that nourish the soul. It is necessary for growth. And by growth I mean internal growth. When man eats, drinks and breathes with the purpose of feeding his soul, he extracts from foods, from the air and from drinks certain substances especially nutritious. But there is a type of food superior to this one and it is the one that impresses us intimately. We all know that worries hinder the digestive process and a worry is an impression. Hepatic upsets produce a sour character. So by feeding ourselves adequately with impressions, whether they be internal or external, we can nourish ourselves better or worse. But this requires studies and efforts. For example, there are those who pray before eating, invoking the blessing of the Highest, but during the meal they chat, discuss or have arguments. During digestion there are those who even throw curses. So they don't have a continuity of purpose. Through continuity of purpose a new organ is formed in man. But it is necessary for the organ to exist potentially for it to be able to grow."

"Which organ is that one?"

"Now you wouldn't understand it because you are convinced that you already have it. Everybody is convinced of the same, as they are convinced of their continuity of purpose. I will only tell you that it is formed in one way and not in two: voluntary suffering and making an effort to follow the voice of the consciousness."

"But everybody suffers."

"No. Sufferings arrive to them as pleasures do. Voluntary suffering presupposes a certain degree of will. One's own will. We all know that hatred is bad and that love is good. We know that we must love our enemies. We know all these things by heart, but we can't put them into practice because we don't have the degree of will enough to put it into practice, so then the society in which we live goes with what it calls human weakness and forgets the principle. To be able to suffer voluntarily it is necessary to have strength to overcome accidental suffering. And this doesn't mean to run off towards pleasures, because those who suffer accidentally also enjoy accidentally. It is necessary to overcome the accidental. And this is only possible through a continuity of purpose, on a clear understanding of many things, the majority of which modern society ignores or despises."

Few times we had such long chats. I would have liked to continue, but he soon changed the topic of the conversation and planned new bicycle rides.

6

A long time passed before we dealt with those issues again. During this time, I wanted to comprehend his words and often revised my notes. But I didn't understand too much. The few times we touched the subject, he avoided going too deeply and, on my part, I stopped taking notes so now it will be impossible to reconstruct loose sentences and explanations that he gave me over many points.

I was especially interested about the food of the soul; but he insisted that, first, it was necessary to wake up.

"What are you trying to tell me with that about waking up?" I asked him one day.

"You still haven't realized?"

"The awakening or the watchfulness that I'm talking about

is difficult but not impossible. It is a continuous effort, a permanent blindfolded walk for a long time until we manage to understand fallacies. But the great moment arrives to who maintains the effort alive. Then is when the latent possibilities within man are noticed. It is something that one knows, one doesn't need to be told or to have it interpreted by anyone. Discovered in the body are different classes of life, different levels. So then one doesn't walk blindfolded anymore. One knows where he is heading and knows the reason why he does everything that he does. The Gospels turn into a very valuable guide. So you see, neither of us can say that we are disciples of a being as magnificent and glorious as Jesus Christ, and believe ourselves to be awake. In the garden of Gethsemane, the apostles, the disciples, remained asleep…"

My friend said these last words with such a reverent tone that it impressed me; his eyes began to fill with tears and he let them run down his cheeks without being ashamed of it. What follows he said in a faltering voice with such powerful emotion that, for an instant, it also shook me. I was puzzled. He continued saying:

"An apostle is by itself a superior man and Jesus was of an intelligence that Earth has seen in few counted times. However, there are those who think that he surrounded himself of idiots and fools. The Apostles had a will against many odds; otherwise they wouldn't have been able to live near Jesus. However, they all failed Jesus in his last days. And that is the history of man's internal development. Ups and downs."

We both remained silence. I didn't want to continue asking him because of fear of causing him new disturbances. He noticed my attitude and said:

"Do not interpret this emotion wrongly; it is not weakness, it is strength. It is the way to obtain a particular understanding."

The way he referred to the intelligence of Jesus and of his

Apostles powerfully caught my attention. For some reason I thought that Judas must have been the same as the others, and I told him.

"First of all," he said, "I need to insist upon a fact. To be a disciple of a figure like Jesus it is necessary to have seen something, to have understood something; it is necessary to know something truly real. Now; it is said that the disciples were fishermen. Jesus tells them that he will make them *'fishermen of men'*. This means that the twelve disciples already possessed some spiritual preparation when they made contact with The Master. If they wouldn't have known something truly real, they wouldn't have been able to recognize the Christ in Jesus, they couldn't have valued correctly his teaching. To gather around Jesus presupposes an intelligence of a certain development, a certain degree of will and a feeling more or less deep of the truth. Naturally everything changed after the crucifixion, but this is another thing. Secondly, to suppose that Judas could have deceived Jesus is almost a blasphemy. The relationship between Christ and his disciples is a relationship that man cannot conceive of in terms of an ordinary life, based in the perceptions that the senses give. That is, to shape the eyes to see and the ears to hear; to see and hear meanings rather than isolated facts; it is to see and to hear in a plane of relationships. It is said that Judas betrayed Jesus, but when the meaning of the facts is captured, it is soon realized that Judas' behaviour wasn't out of his own will; he was obliged to sell Jesus. What *selling* means in the language of the Gospels is related to the poorness or richness in spirit. Only remember that it is said the kingdom of heaven is something very precious that a good merchant finds, and that he soon *sells* everything he owns to be able to have that preciousness. Invert the process to get close to an understanding. The mystery of Judas is one of the mysteries that most confuse us. Jesus knew that he was going to die. More even, he knew how he was going to die. His death was already predetermined, so then there was no room for betrayal, because any betrayal requires the element of a confidence based on ignorance. Think about it a little. Because what Jesus said insists that he chose the twelve and that one was the devil. Looking at the facts retrospectively it is very easy to judge and condemn Judas in base of what others interpret. But to discover the mystery by itself and with the eagerness to know the truth, it is another thing. We all carry a Judas within, as we have a Baptist, a Peter, a John and almost every character that appears in the Gospels. If we understand that these writings are about the internal development of man, we start to see the legion of characters within ourselves, as well as the facts and events that connect them."

Another point that interested me was about love and sexual relations. When I tackled this subject, a few days later than the case before, he said to me:

"Love is the key of everything, because it is the force that keeps and maintains everything. The formula: *'To love God above all things and the neighbour as we love ourselves'* requires a deep consideration. Nobody can love their neighbour more than themselves, but to love oneself requires certain types of impressions a bit difficult to explain. If we see and consider love from the point of view of the impressions, we would see that those who are in love see everything pink. This is a very special food. But when one loves knowingly, when one loves consciously, with complete knowledge, with complete understanding; the delights of the person in love are nothing in comparison with the delights of the love that sprouts only from the spirit. To love oneself is to yearn for internal development and this requires normality. Someone who suffers an inhibition or a frustration can't love himself. So then, to love oneself implies necessarily a normal equilibrium of all functions, including the sexual. But this is difficult to understand unless adultery in love is understood. From this point of view, adultery in love is to have a loving or sexual relationship with someone who one doesn't love completely. And the love must be reciprocal. Only conscious love can produce true love. There is a big difference between to love and to be in love; the first one presupposes a certain degree of self-knowledge and the understanding of certain laws. The second one is something predetermined by nature with the aim of creation and maintenance of life. For a conscious evolution, equilibrium and normality are necessary. This is determined by one's own comprehension. When approaching this issue, the Gospels use the expression *eunuch*. But before indicating this, it is pointed out that the order comes from the internal word. And this is comprehension."

A few days after, my friend gave me a document, a poem, which really grabbed my attention because of the contrast with the aridity of his explicative words, which I have quoted. The poem says:

> *"God gave the Sun the Earth as a wife and blessed that love when He created the Moon.*
>
> *In this way He also created you, woman, to pour His life over human love.*
>
> *And so that in the pleasure of loving the soul finds the path of return to where there is always today, where there is no tomorrow.*
>
> *Because in the same way life goes to death for love, love resurrects from death where there is an awakened heart that knows how to hold it in its love and in its dying.*

With each kiss a bit of the soul dies when it forgets that it is life in love.

And, for the same reason, with each kiss, it can revive the soul of the one who knows how to die.

Oh, Paradox of Creation!

In each breath of love there is a sigh which is eternity.

And in each caress the fire of death and resurrection also burns.

Rise the simple and plain love to the highest summits!

And let loving and kissing be a prayer of life to the most intimate being which is the truth and is God.

Because it is not you who loves, but the love of the Father that shakes within you.

Yours will be his most powerful blessing if in each kiss you give and receive sanctify his name, keeping his presence in your most intimate yearnings.

And in your love, look first for the kingdom of God and his Justice too, as everything else, even the privilege of being, will be given to you as well.

And don't be afraid to love; before be afraid of those who could turn your love into prejudice or evil.

Make of your union a serene path towards the heavens.

While you carry his presence in your hearts, you will be truly loving God above all things as well as loving one another.

And in the instance of your supreme happiness, you will be one with Him and His creation."

I didn't see him again for a while, as he probably went for a long trip. We exchanged a few letters. I remember that in one of them I asked him how I could reach such understanding of life and love. His response arrived in the form of a paradoxical poetry:

> *"Don't doubt of the doubt, and doubt.*
> *But doubt with faith, and even doubt of the faith.*
> *As, isn't the doubt inertia in the slope of the faith towards darkness, and strength in the impulse to reach comprehension?*
> *Do not doubt, and however, doubt of everything which you believe is true, in itself and for itself.*
> *Doubting of the doubt, and doubting with faith and of the faith, you will see the illusion of the doubt and the faith collapse at your feet…and rising majestically in front of your eyes the doubt made Truth."*

7

We met again at the start of the following autumn. I noticed certain changes in him, but I couldn't explain them. He avoided topics relating to the Gospels. Only once, when I told him that I couldn't comprehend how he was so devoted to Jesus Christ and at the same time so into the reading of Maya, Inca, Guarani, Hindu and Chinese works, he made this observation:

"Each town, each race, each nation, each epoch has had messengers that have given testimony of the same and only truth even when they have employed different words, different symbols and different allegories. Words, symbols and allegories don't have a permanent value in themselves; they are only methods that little by little need to be discarded as the understanding and the experience of reality grow. However, for a long time in our lives we cannot see but words within the words and symbols within the symbols. When we observe that two symbols are not the same, little we worry to find out if we are right or not; we believe for a long time that external differences have the same difference internally. But each symbol is a word and each word is a symbol, How many know what they are saying when they say the word *I*?"

To this explanation followed something about the dimensions of time and the dimensions of space. As I indicated, I noted down the majority of things he said. But in this occasion I didn't and I vaguely remember something like space is time, that there are three dimensions of space and three dimensions of time, that the Hebrew symbol of the six pointed star was an indicative symbol that space and time were the same thing or being. If I remember well, on another occasion he also said that the words of Jesus: *'I am the path, the truth and the life,'* could be taken in physics as the three dimensions of time besides constituting a process of cosmic order, which together with another five processes based on the trinity, constitute all the universal processes, in all degrees of the being. But, as I already said, I don't have notes about his words, however I gather that there are writings about it somewhere. Many other things he told me entered through one ear and came out the other.

At this time I was interested in many other things apart from my friendship with him. But our friendship was kept firm. He wasn't a sumptuous man. He dressed well but without luxury. With a bit more dressing he would have been an elegant man. For some reason he tried to dress very discretely and seemed like he didn't want to attract attention; but, as I saw things, he did even if he didn't want to.

Many times I set myself the aim to consider the things that he said. I envied his calmness, his serenity. On the other hand, I was gunpowder one day and a sea of tenderness the next. When I suffered some kind of trouble I couldn't do less than remember his words. We both continued gathering in the same church every afternoon. But as a consequence of the war, my life started to change rapidly, and time started to be briefer. From quick visits, and more sporadic each time to the church, I went to several days of absence. These turned into weeks and soon I realized that I had stopped praying and I had also stopped having the talks with my friend, who I didn't see but when he, without calling, would turn up in my office.

My situation had improved a lot. I was a prosperous man. I had an important position and like every *important* man, I lacked time for many things like, for example, to fulfill my own promise of never failing for one day to go to the temple. I justified myself blaming the war. My importance lay in the fact that everybody was interested in getting promptly informed of the events. Diplomats and politicians knew that they would always find the last minute news on my desk. My phone rang without rest. It was necessary to install a reserved number. Every day, officers from the government, embassies, big commercial firms, etc would visit me or call me. And, as it naturally happens, these professional contacts soon turned into personal friendships. My circle expanded. Inevitably, invitations to parties began to arrive, wines of honor and intimate reunions organized by one or other group. And I, that didn't find time to go for half an hour to church in the afternoons, found that I could attend all these social functions. I always resorted to the excuse: "It is about the war and I owe the public who pays for my services."

One day, when I gave this kind of explanation to my friend, he looked at me with an expression of compassion, and taking a blank notebook from my table, he wrote:

"Never feel so perfect that you let the guard down or ease vigilance."

"Love yourself well, but don't prostitute yourself."

"Keep it where you can see it often, he told me when handling it to me."

Then he stood up and left.

A few months went by without seeing him. I often remembered him. His strange observations, his opportunist advice in matters to which I assumed he was completely ignorant, all this and my own conscience gave me a weird anxiety each time I thought about him or read his words.

At that time commenced the fury of *good neighborhood*. It began the Pan-Americanism fury. The international intrigues, each more mean, flourished everywhere. I could realize that various European potencies, apparently friends with the United States, battled in an underhand way the idea of good neighborhood. Everyone wanted to get a piece out of the benefits that the good war business produced. Neither industry people, nor miners, nor politicians, diplomats or journalists, were free from this temptation. And I also fell into it and fell with much pleasure through a friend who speculated strongly in the Stock Market and who needed to be well informed and timely about the events of the war. Like this I started to become wealthy.

On the other hand, certain propagandist organizations started asking me for collaborations in form of the articles. And they paid even better the more high-sounding and stupid they were. I accepted and gained more money.

A certain time I remembered some observations that my friend had made when the first polls started about the Good

Neighborhood of the United States.

"Good neighbor can only be the one who pays cash. Nowadays no one is in the position of doing so, even less South American countries. But since man lives off beautiful words, and the more beautiful the sillier, he finds that the concept is sonorous, they applaud it and don't know what they are getting into. It is a concept born from the parable of the Good Samaritan. But in the United States someone has distorted it and the rest of the countries have distorted it even more. But the idea is nice and, since in the United States there is plenty of money, there goes the Pan-American parade that is no more than a serpent of 20 mouths and one head."

"This is too caustic," I said.

"The truth is always caustic, especially for the hypocrites. Do not identify so much with the propaganda that you write and you might be able to see some reality."

"But the good neighborhood at least means a good intention."

"Satan has the best intentions with man, that's why he stupefies him."

"You see everything so coldly; the Pan-Americanism is a good intention."

"You sleep still. If you would understand that man couldn't have continuity in his purposes, you will soon understand that the intention is not enough. If man could maintain continuity in his thought, feeling and action, his good intentions would give generous results. In the same way that man has great intentions one day and the next day something takes him away from them, it also happens in politics. The idea of democracy is older than walking by foot, but it is impossible because it requires a discrimination that few have."

Amongst my notes during this time, I find a page from a letter that he wrote to me in regards to international politics of back then, during one of his trips.

It goes like this:

"...Mister Roosevelt is, with no doubt, a man of very good intentions, but it occurs that his sole good neighbor is his cigarette, in the same way that the sole and true ally of Mister Churchill is his cigar and the sole comrade of Mister Stalin is his pipe. Observe that neither Hitler nor Mussolini smoke. They are too virtuous and like every fanatic of virtuosity, they only see the straw in someone else's eye. When this war finishes it is probable that another one takes place and with it maybe science progresses to the extreme of getting the pleasure and enjoying the glory of having destroyed civilization. There is nothing easier than to prophesize a war. But war also includes the uneasiness in life of nations and of the individual itself. If this internal uneasiness would be used by the individual for his development, and if he wanted to find out where does he come from and why he occurs, I believe it would be a step towards peace. But it is not an easy thing to achieve for man, to comprehend that before heavenly phenomenon, he is less than an atom. Peace is an individual conquest; it has never been a conquest of the masses. And even less a labor of the armies. Man still hasn't learned to take advantage of what history teaches, what experience shows. The League of Nations was for many years an illusion of peace; the truth is that it was the focus of intrigues. Mussolini destroyed it with a stroke of the pen. After this war something similar will emerge but with some other name. Man enjoys giving or changing names to the most ancient things in history. The League of Nations was born dead. It had already died in Greece more than two thousand years ago, with the Anfictionia. It is not about organizations; it is not necessary to change names, but it is necessary to change man. Don't ask me to take the good neighborhood seriously because it all adds up to a bunch of lies. The tragedy is that no one lies intentionally, no one realizes the Great Lie. Observe it in yourself, observe how you have already commenced to believe in all the lies you are writing."

Of all this, what interested me was the idea that a good neighbor can only be the one who pays cash. I decided to use the idea for an article and when I published it, my life suffered a new transformation connected, in a way, with this singular friend.

I saw myself fully thrown into intrigues of political espionage.

A few days after elaborating this idea in a series of articles, I saw myself in contact with certain sellers of machinery that couldn't be fabricated anywhere else. I met them through some diplomatic friends. And since then my importance grew. All of a sudden, I saw that even my opinion was *important*. Even the biggest nonsense I used to say, when I had a bit more alcohol in the body, began to have importance. The importance and the consideration that I was given rested neither in my intelligence, nor in my critical judgment, as it had been a long time since I used any of these functions. It rested simply in the position I fulfilled and continued to fulfill as long as I followed the emptiness of my *importance*.

It is worthless to tell my story in the middle of all the intrigues from that time. I cite only the facts that have a relation to my friend and his ideas. But what I could observe in the politicians, diplomats and spies with whom I socialized, would give place to a beautiful humorist comedy if it wouldn't be for the tragic consequences that the activities of these fauna and flora of our culture brought about. I observe that I am writing with certain resentment, and I do not hide it. And if my friend could read this now, he would surely say something more or less like this:

"You haven't learned how to forgive. You are still asleep.

Your flora and your fauna can't stop or mutilate your life."

By writing this I notice how much nostalgia I feel for him, how sad is not to be beside him now. But let's come back to the story.

One night he invited me for dinner. My confidence hadn't diminished. We chatted for a long time and with great joy. I told him my observations and he smiled with fondness and understanding as meaning: "poor people, it's not their fault." After dinner we went together to my apartment that differed a lot from that simple room I had lived in for so many years before becoming *important*. He looked at everything in silence. Remembering that night, I see how dull my behavior was. I started to show him proudly all my possessions; the stock market share titles, the clothes, a cute miniature bar, my sporty corner with a punching bag, a punching-ball, boxing gloves, the iron levers, and my beautiful Italian bicycle. When I finished my exhibition, I said to him with proud tone:

"What do you think?"

"Perfect." he said. "You have little to go to become a complete cretin. I'm not referring to this, to the commodity, but to your attitude towards all this comfort and to the harm you are causing yourself."

"I don't understand you," I said to him. "I earn enough money; I live well and enjoy life."

"To what price?"

"I don't find it so terrible" I protested. "Don't be prudish. The only thing left for you to do is to censure the traces of woman that you have found."

"Maybe they are the traces of the only decent thing left within you. But it is your life. Live it as you want."

I felt a vague fear hearing him saying these words. We kept a silence for a while. Then, I felt a strong desire to confess to him everything that was torturing me.

"I need help," I said.
"I'm listening."

I explained to him all the things that had turned into a dreadful dilemma within me, that infernal circle of lies which I had fallen into. He listened with great attention and asked me some questions so I could clear up certain points that I didn't want to expose openly. He reflected for an instant when I finished.

"What do you have to say?" I asked him.
"What do you want me to say?"
"What I need to do."
"Cut from the root, break out from everything. Leave all this and start again."
"But, are you crazy?"
"No; you are the crazy one. Look at what you have reached to."

And going towards the bathroom, he pulled out of the closet a bottle which contained pills of a stimulant with which I needed to activate daily my nervous system to be able to maintain such a train of life.

When I saw him with the bottle in his hand I realized a lot of things, of his amazing power of observation, of his real goodness and of the fondness he professed towards me. But I felt that things had gone too far away to change them. I put my head down in silence.

"Thank goodness you have left a bit of shame," he told me. "Take advantage of it and take up again the course of your life before it finishes completely. Soon you will go from this stimulant to drugs. And, when you feel the need to run away from the rubbish you live in, the punch bag and the boxing gloves will disappear and you will put in their place pornographic pictures. Now, that love that you have in your life can help you, but if you don't understand it, if you don't stick to it with all your strength, if you continue to give in to temptation in this way, you will lose love and look for orgies."

"You know well that I can't leave my work. You know what it is all about, You know that it is the war."

"That's up to you. You asked me what you should do and I have answered you. I have nothing else to tell you."

Then it was when I committed the lamentable error:

"Listen" I said to him. "You are more intelligent than I am. I will give you half of what I have and of what I earn if you help me to come out of this."

He looked at me in silence, without saying a word. I realized too late how I had hurt him. I saw how tears showed in his eyes. He went away overwhelmed by a singular sadness and when he was already at the door, he said:

"Thirty pieces of silver…"

I felt like saying sorry to him, but something stopped me. I went to the bar and while I was serving myself a glass of whisky, I remembered that other silent scene that seemed to have happened in a past too distant already, that time, in the church, when I had exclaimed 'shit' and he had answered 'amen'. I drank the whisky in one go, I looked to the stimulant tablets that he had left on the bar counter, and I said in loud voice:

"He can go to hell!"

I drank whisky until intoxicated.

8

Time went by.

All of a sudden, the machine I was caught up into started to function in a different way, more intensively. We were approaching the end of the war. Everything was more desperate. I changed cities, I went to another country and there I had to continue what I had started and of which I couldn't escape anymore. I remembered my friend only from time to time.

Each day I found more amazing the easiness with which I lied and deceived, and the facility with which everybody seemed to believe my lies and deceits.

One night that I had drunk more than what I needed to forget my dirtiness, I found my friend.

He looked at me in silence and without letting me express my happiness, he told me:

"Reflect a bit. Don't look for sufferings you don't need."

I knew that I couldn't lie to him. I asked him not to leave me and he announced that he was going to stay in that city for a while and that we would probably see each other regularly.

We talked very little that night. It didn't stop intriguing me what he said, that I was looking for sufferings that I didn't need. But, as usual, I thought it would be a new extravagance on his behalf. On the other hand, I would have liked to demonstrate a greater hospitality and, in general, respond to his devotion as a friend in a more tangible manner. When I offered him my house to stay, he declined politely informing me that his trip had been arranged by other friends, and that he had already promised to stay with them, but that we would see each other often.

In our next interview I asked him if he had read my articles and he responded yes and that he had cut some to keep. This caught my attention strongly. I was expecting for him to say something like: "I don't read political propaganda", etc. But, that he had cut one of my articles was truly a novelty. I asked him which article. He pulled it out of his wallet.

I was expecting for it to be one of those speculations full of complexity that tried to present an international picture, citing the magnates of banks and the union leaders, etc. But what my friend had cut was something very different: a comment about certain Guarani songs where I presented my own impressions.

"It is very important what you have observed in this music" he said to me. "It corresponds faithfully to a treasure of wisdom that the Guarani still feels but has stopped understanding, overwhelmed by the occidental culture. I find in it the same as in all the folklore of the continent: the string hidden in time. Read this little Yucateca work and you will see the same content however in a different way."

And he gave me a book that I still keep.

He told me that that article was what had induced him to find me again and he added:

"You cannot imagine how much good you did to yourself by listening to that music with so much attention. It will always vibrate within you."

I smiled and answered:

"Well…if you want Guarani music, I have plenty at home. I also have two beautiful Maya songs and a lot of records of Inca music."

I explained to him in detail how I had gathered this collection and even mentioned the amounts I had spent on it. He listened to me pleased.

"The Guarani has a very rich expression that means that everything that the man says in words, in human language, is a portion of the substance of the soul; you would notice that this concept is similar to one of the holy truths of Christianity when it states that of the richness of the heart the mouth speaks. And there are those who have said that man can only express what he is. Anyway…"

The following night we had dinner at my house and stuffed ourselves with Guarani music. But I was agitated and nervous due to the events of the day and would have preferred to discuss my personal problems with him. He listened to the music in delight. I was drinking whisky. The music was certainly attractive but I had my head full of worries due to my life being in the middle of so much intrigue. My situation was getting too dense and it seemed not to have a single crack from where to escape. In that instant I envied the calmness of my friend, the immeasurable peace that he had within and, especially, his security, his assurance.

When he stood up, just before leaving, he said to me:

"The Guarani has done more or less the same as you are doing with that glass of whisky; they drink 'caña.' It is not completely unpleasant, but to drink it to escape from oneself is the most foolish thing a man can do. The Guarani has fallen into the same net of drowsiness in which you have fallen. That music that we just listened to is the voice of their soul captured by a man that wants to still wake up his own people. The Voice of Life still vibrates in them, but they have let themselves get hypnotized not only by alcohol but by the occidental encyclopaedia which is the poison that consumes our people."

"I don't think anything has died in the Guarani" I said to

him. "His virility is something clear. I believe that the Guarani is the bravest man I have ever met; I saw it in the war. And, by the way, it was during the war that I got to know his music and I find it as beautiful and eloquent as the Andean Music."

"Yes; they are both genuine called from the soul of these lands, but the forms are different because they correspond to different latitudes. Both are essentially mystic music. The one of Inca origin follows the rhythm of the celestial bodies and it can't be any other way; it is music that contains in its rhythm and in its melody, everything which our soul already knows about the solar system and the unknown of the Milky Way and the Pleiades. At more than three thousand meters above the sea level, the man of the Andes has to inevitably feel in grandiose terms. If their thought would be at the same height as their feelings, the race wouldn't have degenerated. This degeneration began long before the conquest; even then, their degeneration is proportionally less than the occidental one in regards to Christianity. This can be observed in the writings that survived the catholic conversion of the Empire. The souls of this race still have enough spiritual strength; but unfortunately, they don't know how to bring it up to date and have hid it in the depths of the catholic practices. In regards to the Guarani, the semi-tropical nature in which he lives gives him another rhythm, another form, another feeling; but in essence, it says the same spiritually. It happens that very few men understand the reality of life through the feelings, through the emotions, and that has produced a civilization of schizophrenics. What has been called the subconscious, it is nothing but correlative functions that can operate harmoniously with the mind, with the thoughts. That's why I tell you that if all that artistic treasure, if this emotional expression was understood intellectually, the races of our continent would understand their true destiny. But there are already those who work to give light in this sense. For the moment these men are like John the Baptist - a voice that cries in the desert."

"As you are telling me, it would be good to revive the religions and myths of the autochthonous races," I said to him.

"No; that would be silly. In that sense there is nothing to revive because nothing has died. We can't go to the forms of the past; we can only comprehend the eternal principle that animates all forms. We have to comprehend, not disintegrate or divide. And this is a task for each individual."

"It has been calculated that there are ten million Indians in South America. An audacious man who knows their language could organize them and rise them to revolt. It would be interesting."

He looked at me compassionately.

"You see," he said, "there, in yourself, you have the occidental schizophrenia. You have saturated yourself with so much violence that you can't measure life but in terms of destruction and of death."

Several days went by without seeing each other. Around that date the matters of my life were getting complicated incredibly. The machine was catching me inexorably and I was feeling like a little bird hypnotized by a snake, knowing that I was going to die, that has to run away but cannot do it. When I saw my friend again, I trusted to him the facts.

"It is already too late" he told me. "Now you have to follow the movement of the machine where it carries you. You can't run away. Look."

And directing me to a window facing the street, he pointed out two men that were trying to hide their presence.

"Who are they?" I asked.

"You are so self-satisfied with your success that you haven't realized things. Falsehood has you trapped. They are policemen who have been following you for several days."

I felt a punch in the heart. I don't get frightened easily, and if I know fear well, I also know that courage is precisely to dominate it no matter how intensively they are hounding us. But something inside of me was trembling horrified before the crude fact that it was reaching its end. I looked at my friend waiting for him to say something, but he just said:

"You should be intimately grateful that this exit is presented before you. Generally for the type of intrigues that you have got yourself into, the exit is suicide or…an accident in the street."

He didn't make major comments. He knew me well enough to know that I wasn't going to commit suicide. And in regards to the street accident I remained cold. I knew that I was a danger for many and that many would see my disappearance with pleasure. But I had anticipated this possibility and had let every one of them know that I carried a diary were I noted things that the political and diplomatic world called 'very interesting.' There were several copies of that diary, some of them abroad, and others in a bank.

I told these things to my friend.

"A trapped rat always has talent," he told me.

I turned to him with violence and had my fist high to hit him, but his look paralyzed me. Even now I can't explain how that happened. He didn't move a finger, he didn't make a single gesture. He only looked at me and I was disarmed inside and outside.

"You are so rotten that you have lost your integrity" he told me. "How much you have changed! Once you revealed to me the way you used to pray in the church. Do you remember? No matter how silly and childish those words were, at least your integrity and your honesty were of value. Now…look at yourself."

9

The remembrance of those days so remote in my memory, to see them surface in front of me in that situation, in those conditions, shook me. Without being able to avoid it I started to cry like a boy. In that moment I realized how much I loved my friend, how much he meant to me. He went to another room while I let my tears run in a corner. When I recomposed myself I went looking for him and found him on his knees, with his arms in the shape of a cross and looking towards the firmament through the open window.

Without demonstrating the least embarrassment, he stood up and, looking at me, he said:

"Crying is a good purgative; it purifies the blood."

He went towards the bathroom and I saw him washing his face with cold water. He had also been crying.

During that winter the country's situation got exceedingly rough. I was linked too tightly to the war. But it was in spring when the events took sanguinary proportions and certain things that occurred determined my detention by the police and I was taken to prison.

It would be convenient to register some of the observations made by my friend that relate with the events of back then, even though he affirmed that neither of the things that happened were new.

I had clearly noticed the increasing strength that the supposed dictator of that country was gaining; he was making a comedy to exploit the feelings of the masses that followed him blindly by virtue of a few circumstantial benefits that they had received. My articles outlined these facts, but my bosses complained and accused me of being a supporter of the man. There was violence. They wanted a more active opposition in my writings and they didn't seem capable of understanding the need to say the truth and face the obvious reality that we were witnessing. When I commented these facts to my friend, he said:

"The only thing that really has importance in all this mess is that the Feathered Serpent wants to fly already, but has its legs shackled to the ground."

"Please, don't answer me with enigmas."

"There is no enigma in this. If instead of wasting your time in childishness you would have caught the thread of some of the indications I gave you from time to time, you would have studied something transcendental, and you would understand the huge significance that the Feathered Serpent has for you."

"All this is very good," I said to him, "but it doesn't explain the reason why my bosses are so obtuse that they don't want to see the reality of the situation in this country."

"It is because they are serpents without wings and without feathers."

"Surely you could tell me things more clearly."

"I don't want to tell you things more clearly. The truth is always bitter for the sleeping one, because it takes him out of his drowsiness."

"You have been telling me the same for years and I still don't understand."

"Because you still sleep."

As the winter moved forward, my articles started to attract various individuals from other countries. The general situation seemed uncertain. Other countries were receiving contradictory information. But one event about which I informed in detail determined a new form of relationship with politicians and diplomats who were arriving in pursuit of correct information. The event was that the supposed dictator, following the accurate advice of his chief of police, made a raid of every person in the opposition that stood out, including doctors, directors of big newspapers, lawyers of international renown, etc. All those who directed the movement of freedom of thought and other types of freedom that my friend classified, summarizing them, as 'the freedom of dreaming awake'. In regards to the political chiefs, my friend said that they were a collection of Pilots who could not be any other thing except in the instances where, in the human comedy, they changed roles and were Herods who, in more than one opportunity, had been obliged to please the vanities of the different types of Salome, and slaughter more than one honest Baptist.

The facts confirmed more than enough my friend's words. However, to balance the situation, I will cite my friend's opinion about the dictator and his people:

"Those are the ones that sleep the most and the best," he used to say. "They dream that they dominate the masses and they don't have enough discernment to observe that they shout Hosanna! with the same ease as they shout crucify Him!"

But it is by all known how the end of the war confirmed all this.

The fact was that the democratic leaders waited patiently in prison for the masses to come and rescue them, but no one moved a finger for their cause. More even, everybody applauded the dictator euphorically for having dared to touch the untouchables. This event confused the politic and diplomatic comprehension of everyone.

It was obvious that this dictator, like many others,

intuitively knew the passions of the masses and exploited them very well. The opposition was completely destroyed, but even like this, few realized the truth. There were many editorials, many protests, but it was uproar and no more than uproar.

My articles, that to some extent reflected the opinions of my friend, started to call the attention and attracted the men who I already indicated. One day, one of them arrived and I informed him in detail. This confidential correspondent, however, sent to his government a report several pages long to end up saying that it was convenient to delay a decision, that everything was still uncertain. When he came back, two months later, he informed his own people again that it was still necessary to delay any decision.

This irritated me.

"Why do you deceive your government?" I asked him.

The man didn't even feel upset, or offended. He looked at me very pleased and told me:

"I also see the situation like you. But we happen to be also on the verge of election and our situation is still not clear so I don't know the position that I am going to adopt yet. So-and-so" and he cited the name of a governor, "doesn't have any sympathy for so-and-so" - the name of the dictator - "and has, however, a good chance to be the next president of our country. Since he occupies an outstanding position I sent him a copy of the report so, as presumptive leader, he can be ahead of the facts. A finished report, like your articles are, would only serve for him to forget my services. On the other hand, with several reports I prepare the possibility of getting assigned the embassy of this country. You, my friend, would be a dreadful diplomat."

This was a case. There were others. Directly opposite to this one was of the correspondent of a country whose situation was similar to mine. He moved quickly to make contact with the men of the dictator; he didn't hide his sympathy for him and offered to buy from me all the material that I had accumulated. He believed all I said. And in this light he issued a report, of which he gave me a copy, full of the most fantastic affirmations I have ever read in my entire career. I had lied myself to please my readers. But the report of this diplomat exceeded all fantasy and reality together. It seemed the tale of One Thousand and One Nights.

Immediately after, he made me a series of propositions of commercial nature. It wasn't the first time that I found people who hid the facts to speculate with them.

"Do you think that anyone from your government would believe this?" I said to him.

"Don't worry about that, my friend," he answered. He was a nice, pleasant man, shameless to satiety; but I couldn't condemn him. We were both trapped within the machine.

My amazement was great when I found out that his government had accepted his report and was acting based on it. I could never explain to myself how men, who seemed skillful in the matters of the state, could have their gullets as open as any other ingenuous.

This confidential correspondent, before returning to his country, gave me a fine wallet full of notes and when I wanted, weakly, to turn it down, he said to me:

"By no means, dear friend. You have helped me in a magnificent business."

Later I found out that the business was a strong smuggling of raw materials, very scarce for the industry due to the war.

I told all the facts to my friend.

"That is the oldest trick in the world," he said. "They are not to blame. They are irresponsible. But you worry about not shackling the Feathered Serpent. Remember that you can't serve two masters."

Once again I ignored his sensible advice. The events took speed. The police watched over me each time more closely and with the hope to save myself in some way, I started to participate in a lot of conspiracies against the dictator.

10

In the middle of spring, with the good weather, a wave of violence burst out every where, in every country. Students started to riot instigated by the democratic leaders that the police had humiliated. These were throwing written manifests one after another comfortably from an elegant club. One day I had an interview with them after some events where several students fell prisoners and were injured. I informed them of the facts.

"What barbarity!" they exclaimed. "Where is this man going to lead us?"

"You know perfectly well," I told them. "You must act now."

"But, what can we do?"

"If you are afraid of going out to the street and face the killers and police, at least don't incite those kids any more."

"It is because the patriotic love burns in their blood," a banker said.

"Go to hell, faggots!" I exclaimed with all the fury that consumed me those days. I went home and my friend was waiting for me. I told him the incident.

"The Feathered Serpent wants to fly" was all his answer.

I wasn't in the mood for those things. I turned my back to him and went to my room. Once I calmed down, I found him going over the notebook where I noted down his comments and observations. He was correcting some things.

"You are a good journalist and you have good memory," he told me. "You have committed few errors."

Of every noteworthy thing of my friend I had not only taken down his words, but I had described the scene with an abundance of details, names, places, dates, etc. He asked me to destroy every personal reference, everything that was a place, a date, a name. I left only those facts that could portray him, and of those notes comes out this story.

Many of the spies and secret agents with whom I had contact escaped on time. Enemies of these agents, at the service of another country, also started to watch closer over me. There was no doubt now that my game was in the open. One day I found out that some of the spies who knew me were in prison. As usual, I trusted everything to my friend and he said to me:

"Those who are in prison have given you away; those who escaped have spoken in other countries. And these other ones are using you."

"What to do?" I said to him.

"Recover your manhood. Or give yourself in openly and tell all the truth, or continue until the end and wait for whatever comes."

"I will continue until the end," I said with the hope that something would happen in my favor.

I started to feel a certain repugnance towards myself, and trusted this to my friend.

"It is natural," he said. "The dream turns into nightmare because the effect of the psychic drugs that you have been taking during all this time is starting to dissipate. But don't despair. One day you will discover the big secret of confession and its value, and then you will know that the Feathered Serpent can fly."

It was in those days when I discovered that my friend was a consummate actor, that he could modify his appearance almost at will and that he could transform himself into whoever he wanted. The incident that allowed me to discover this new finding started one night when some politicians, who I was in close contact with in the conspiracy, called me with great urgency. We arranged a meeting far from the city center. When I was coming out of my house, agitated about the urgent tone with which they had called me, I encountered my friend:

"Something serious is happening. So-and-so has called me. Come with me," I said to him.

The problem was that one of the conspirators, director of a newspaper of battle and who had back then a quite significant circulation, had received a confidential warning. That same night he was going to get arrested and imprisoned. He didn't doubt the veracity of the warning. It had been given to him by one of the policemen who were going to take an active part in the matter. This policeman owed the director certain favors of consideration and also was getting a salary from the conspiracy group. The problem was in helping the director to escape and we considered that his escape could be used towards propaganda goals. The immediate thing was, however, to make him disappear before the police captured him. We were discussing several plans when my friend intervened:

"He could appeal to the right of asylum," he said.

It was a valuable indication. I ran to the telephone and called a diplomatic friend. I was about to tell him our intentions when my friend covered my mouth with his hand and advised me:

"Tell him to go immediately to his embassy, and to leave the door open because you will be arriving by car."

So I did. This diplomat was one of the people who had benefited with my things, so he agreed easily.

The director, my friend and I came out from the meeting. We caught a taxi and when I was about to give the address of the embassy, my friend gave a completely opposite address. We traveled for half an hour, in silence. We stopped in a night bakery. Only when we were sitting down at a table I realized the reason why my friend was taking such precautions. The police had followed us. There were two agents who couldn't hide their identity. I saw how one of them was phoning. My friend also saw him and said:

"They can't dare to act on their own. They are asking for help. Now we are going to use a very old trick."

Saying this, he stood up and went to the men's room. We followed him. In one of the toilets, he swapped clothes with the director. They both were more or less of the same build. We then made a deliberately suspicious exit, one by one, while the police agents looked at us. The three of us met in a corner and saw the two agents coming towards us with awful camouflage. When they were fairly close, my friend started a comedy in such natural way that I almost fell backwards. He did a showy goodbye making an appointment to meet us the next day in such place at such time.

I was perplexed. My friend had imitated to perfection the voice and the accent of the director of the newspaper. He even walked in the same way. He went close to the pavement, called a taxi and left. In a matter of minutes, we saw how the agents went after him.

The director of the newspaper and I were amazed. He said:

"Very noble gesture from your friend. Who is he?"

I didn't respond. When I saw the police going after him, a very singular fear invaded me. I was too well informed of the police methods to ignore his fate if they managed to capture him. I also started to feel a crushing anger against this journalist that was now safe and free of the danger of getting tortured by the police. However, they would not only maltreat my friend mistaking him at the beginning with the director, but they would end up knowing the truth of the facts the next day when embassy X notified the government about the director that had been given asylum.

While I was thinking about all these things, this man that was with me chatted in the most unbearable way. I wasn't paying him attention. But I caught a sentence with which he finished a speech:

"The fight for the freedom of press is indeed bitter."

This sentence hit me in such way that I couldn't help but feel an indescribable scorn towards all the conspirators of this type, men that always used somebody else's feelings to come out well and safe and then grow at the expense of someone else's sacrifice.

"Faggot!" I screamed at him full of anger.

"What did you say?" he asked me amazed.

I grabbed him by the lapels, put him against the wall, and poured on him all the hatred contained in my mind, I said to him:

"I said that you are a faggot. I say now to you and all your collection of faggots that you can go to hell with your freedom of press. My friend has nothing to do with this rubbish. That I put myself at risk is not important because I am with all of you merely to see the way to save myself. I'm as rotten and hypocritical as you. But I don't fool myself any more. And if I help you now is because I need to help myself. What I should do is break your face and give you up to the police so they can finish you off. I'm worried about my friend and not you and your stupidities. Come on, idiot; there in the embassy coffee, cognac, cigarettes await you and a comfortable bed where you can dream with all the glory that I'm going to fabricate for you with the article I will write on this."

The strange thing was that, at the same time as rage, I was feeling certain compassion towards this man. He was part of that legion of deluded people at the start of the revolution who considered it impossible that a mercenary could take possession of power. What irritated me the most was that he was locked in the dream that the people were going to defend what until now was traditional in that country and that nobody had dared to touch. But already the facts had shook him.

When we were in a taxi, I made sure that no one was following us. In any case, for more security, we changed taxis several times. During these maneuvers he started to show signs of fear and wanted to establish a conversation. I said to him abruptly:

"Shut up!"

"But..."

I didn't let him continue. We took the first taxi that went by, and went to embassy X.

"Do you have money with you?" I asked the director.

He pulled out his wallet and said to me:

"How much do you need?"

"All that," I said and took the wallet out of his hand.

"I'm going to remain without a cent."

"But without a scratch on your body and with a crown of laurels. Pay something at least. You can obtain money anywhere. This money will go to those youngsters who have lost their freedom and even their health because of you."

"You are on so-and-so's side" he told me naming the dictator.

"Think whatever you like. Nothing matters to me anymore."

I presented him to the embassy. I checked with the officers to see to what point I could extend my writings. We made an agreement and I wrote it right there. I was very happy when the ambassador told me that in accordance with international law, I couldn't include an interview with the refugee. I felt pleased about this; at least the amount of lies that I was writing about him was reduced. I had portrayed him as a hero, as an audacious man who had managed to outwit the dictator's henchmen.

The ambassador of X, one of the few sober and sensible men in that country, smiled when I showed him my article.

"Why don't you earn your life writing detective novels?" he said to me.

In that moment a boy arrived with coffee, cognac, cigarettes and sandwiches. A few minutes later, the ambassador's secretary arrived with the refugee. He looked at me reproachfully and I realized that he knew about the incident and about the money. He asked to have a word with the ambassador, but I stepped in first:

"Mister Ambassador," I said to him. "A friend who I love very much is now probably in the hands of the police so this man could be saved. This individual is only news for me, nothing else. In the taxi I took his money. Here it is," and I put the wallet on a table. "I haven't counted it, but I am going to keep it and the way I use it is my business. In this article you have seen how I say that this man, in a final gesture, gave a great sum of money to help the cause and those who fight for freedom. Well, I'm going to turn that fame into a literal truth. You are witness that this man is now giving this donation voluntarily."

The ambassador was uncomfortable and annoyed. The secretary was surprised with my audacity. The refugee was looking at me with mouth open, but the most surprised of all was myself. I don't want to justify myself denigrating those revolutionaries of saloon, but I can't stop mentioning that they made me feel an unbearable revulsion. And this revulsion was extending towards myself. I did realize that I was hitting a fallen man, a man who had trusted his life and his freedom to my hands. My feelings were extremely contradictory. I looked at him threatening and with a tone of voice that I had never suspected in me, I said to him:

"Well...what do you say?"

And he, starting a bit clumsy, looked at the ambassador and said to me:

"I understand that the sudden decision of your friend has disturbed you. Of course, I forgive you for the way you have treated me. You are a noble person who is trying to hide his nobility. Have this money and allow me to thank you for everything."

He extended his hand. I felt such repugnance that I struggled to reach him with my own hand. I felt dirty inside, dirty of heart. And it seems like I spoke this within myself:

"I said that I am anything but noble and disinterested. I am as much a liar and as rotten as you. At least let's not be hypocrites."

The ambassador intervened at that moment:

"If I wouldn't know you, I would ask you to leave at once. You are disturbed. Don't drink anymore. In regards to your friend, even if the gentleman gave himself in to the police, nobody can help him. I certainly can't do it without turning my government into an open supporter of his acts. Let's bring this matter to an end. Officially I only know that the gentleman came to ask for asylum and I have granted it to him. Besides this, I don't know anything else."

We exchanged half a dozen phrases required by protocol. The refugee left with the secretary. The ambassador closed the door and we remained by ourselves. We chatted for a long while about things that don't relate to this story. When we said good bye, he said:

"The only thing I ask you is not to turn the embassy into a hotel. We have already gone through this in Spain and I am a bit old for these things."

That night I couldn't sleep pondering about my friend's luck. I tried to place a spy we had in the police force; I didn't manage to locate him. But the following morning, first thing, my friend presented himself at my house. My eyes were irritated because of the lack of sleep and for the excess of alcohol that I had drunk during the whole night. His smile gave me life, I put my arms around him and I was almost about to cry from happiness. But he calmed me with his tranquil:

"Don't lose your head."

We prepared coffee. Before breakfast he made me have an aspirin and advised me:

"It wouldn't be bad if you have a Turkish bath. It would be interesting to see that fatty policeman perspire beside us."

He was referring to an agent that was following my steps.

I told him everything that happened the night before and I was waiting for his reproach, but the only thing he said was:

"You have already started to realize that the freedom that everyone talks about is a myth fabricated by themselves and for themselves. You have started to be sincere with yourself. What you feel now as a reproach is exactly the very beginning of freedom."

"But I have robbed his money; I have abused your condition. I have enough money, and also I have left the ambassador in an uncomfortable situation."

"Sometimes we know a lot from the heart, but our mental ineptitude distorts everything. But it doesn't matter. The interesting part is that you haven't hidden behind some high-sounding sentence to justify your violence. In regards to the ambassador, don't worry. He has seen you as I see you. He is one of us."

"Who are *us*? What is it all about?" I said to him.

"You will get to know them with time. The one who has eyes to see always recognizes his own. On the other hand, you will need that money."

11

I think that my friend could tell the future. None of his forecasts had failed until now. This one neither. The moment news spread about what I had done, about helping the director to run away, my life suffered another unexpected turn. The obscure part of my conduct, naturally, remained in silence. The city's riots were increasing. Students disturbed with one strike after another one. One day two arrived to my home. My friend helped me to make them run away to a neighboring country. He took the money that I had taken away from the director, who was already writing about his heroism abroad and his fantasy exceeded mine by far and divided it between us both. I was stunned to see him taking charge of the situation and to hear him saying that I must now dedicate myself to misleading the police so he can have his hands free in this task.

We soon had to rent an apartment in another part of the city. For several weeks we both played Scarlet Pimpernel. My money ran out quickly. The petrol was rationed, but my friend managed to get coupons. We used diplomatic and attorney vehicles for our enterprise. When I saw that the money was running out I started to obtain it through threats to the gentlemen of the aristocratic club where they were still planning the way to give *moral support* to these students. The spies with who I still maintained links added to our enterprise and even contributed with money. My friend assumed the effective and real direction of the whole system which was starting up very fast. He had such an inconspicuous way of doing things, that no one would have thought that he elaborated all the plans.

For my part, my nerves were destroyed. My friend limited himself to observing me. I increased the dosage of stimulants to keep myself awake and active. During the day I had to carry out my function as a journalist as though nothing abnormal had happened. At night I had to help my friend. I learnt a lot of things out of necessity. One day, in one relaxed hour that we had to chat, I told my friend how badly I felt inside, how much repugnance this life of deceitfulness, lies and sudden shocks produced within me. He limited himself to smiling.

A few days after, the hour of disillusion arrived.

One morning, towards the end of summer, a police party arrived at my house. One of them - while the others searched my drawers, cut the telephone and carried out their job to isolate me - prepared breakfast for everyone. They were all very kind, very courteous. Only one was sitting down on the couch with a machine gun in his hand. The extraordinary thing is that before all this, I started to feel relaxed, serene. And I said to the armed policeman:

"Friend, put away your gun. I assure you that I'm too tired to resist or even to try to run away."

My house remained in the hands of the police. I ended up in a police station where they put me through the most absurd questioning I had ever seen. Judging by the way they were asking questions, and judging by the questions themselves, it seemed that they needed to make a case so sensational to serve as the base for something equally sensational. They were about to persuade me that I was the most dangerous being who ever existed. But I didn't have any kind of resistance, neither internal nor external. Lacking stimulants, my nervous system rested. I said yes to everything, and didn't bother to negate anything. The charges were so fantastic, that I was signing one declaration after another without even reading them.

12

Like this my life ended. My career also. I hoped to see myself involved in some of those scandalous articles similar to the ones I had written many times. And I laughed. I thought that it would be fair to serve as the theme sometime and it didn't worry me at all what I well knew the diaries were going to say about me, nor what my colleagues were going to think. I couldn't give a damn about anything. I only wanted to rest.

But the police took care of stopping the scandal in time. Through my friend, some time after, I found out that they ordered the diaries to say that I wasn't arrested and that I was possibly on holidays somewhere. The true reason for this decision only I knew, but it is such a shady matter, that it doesn't belong in this story, and in this matter my friend didn't intervene at all.

During the first days of isolation in a cell, I tried to remember many of the things my friend had said and that I had noted down. But I didn't have my notebook handy. I started to see life and human things in a very curious way, as if I was isolated from them. This was due to a moment where I remembered something that he had said about the key of The Sermon of the Mountain, of a key that was occult in the first sentences: 'And seeing the crowds, he went up the mountain'.

My disillusions, and everything that had contributed to this, could that be 'to see the crowds' that my friend spoke about? And what would be 'to go up the mountain?' I thought that the mountain would be something like the internal calmness that invaded me as I remembered my friend, a calmness as if I knew that he would give me the answer to all my questions that I was starting to formulate. By the way, in this isolation I could see the revolution, my career, my years of youth, how useless had been my agitated existence and that such a life couldn't lead anywhere, that it didn't have meaning.

I couldn't explain what had happened to the feelings of those students, which scared before the police danger had arrived to my house looking for help. I couldn't explain to myself how it was possible that now and voluntarily they were speaking against me in the indictment.

Eventually I was sent to a prison and remained in peace.

The first visit of my friend occurred in the presence of an interrogation officer. I asked him about my friends, and his answer was typical:

"Here I am," he said to me.

"I'm not referring to you, but to Tom, Dick and Harry, etc."

He looked at me compassionately, and with a false tone he answered:

"Them? They are free men. They are enjoying a wonderful nap."

"I image they are doing well."

"The only one that is doing really well is you. But you still don't understand this."

And addressing the interrogation officer, he said:

"This man needs rest. Above all, he needs to reflect. Could you help him? Since you have studied philosophy some of your words might be useful to him."

I ignored what previous conversations my friend had had with this policeman. The fact was that they seemed close friends. The policeman, clearing his throat and with the tone of a lecturer that it is going to reveal the mystery of life, started to speak about such a pile of emptiness that I had to mask my laugh by lighting up a cigarette. I couldn't dare look at my friend's eyes. The speech finished more or less in the following manner:

"We serve the estate for the good of the community. The Country is above all. But we are also humans. You have confessed. You have saved us work and money. While the authorities pass judgment on your case, I will make sure that you have a good time. Political crimes deserve our gentlemanly consideration. This is like a boxing match: you have lost, we have won. That is all."

His hypocrisy was repulsive. I had seen some of the student's faces that had come to my place looking for help. And I realized that my friend, in some way, had influenced this man so he would convince himself with his own words.

The policeman brought out a chess game. He asked for coffee for everyone and the game commenced. It lasted several hours and I could see that my friend was playing a comical game; he feigned striving to win, but he lost deliberately. At the end, the policeman said to him:

"We must play again. What a struggle to beat you!"

The man was radiant. During the game I had seen him going pale often. At the end, he said very kindly:

"We have to celebrate this victory. I urge you to accept my invitation to a dinner."

My friend looked at me before responding, but the policeman added:

"We will go with him also; but it would be good if you

gave you word of honor that you will not try to escape."

My friend said:

"I will answer for him."

Penal food was odious, so I enjoyed the idea of a dinner in a good restaurant. The policeman took out of the draw of his bureau a little metal safe box where I always had a good sum of cash and that the police had confiscated 'for the investigation.' I saw him putting a hand full of notes in his pocket.

The three of us ate well and happily. My friend was a completely different person. He seemed to admire this policeman like a kid admires his father. A conversation struck up between the policeman and I. Seeing him so vain, I said to him:

"Look, my career as a journalist has ended thanks to you. But I think I have discovered a possibility for the future. Tell me your most interesting investigations and putting that together with the records that I have from the secret service, I could write a good adventure book. This is a type of literature little developed in our countries."

"I will think about it," he told me gravely. After a moment, he added: "Yes, I think you could do it well. I have read your writings and I like your style."

"Thank you," I said to him.

"How would you describe me?"

"Well…it would be necessary first to disfigure your name, true? But to do it in such way that it would be known who we are talking about. Then we would have to modify the description of your appearance. Those are important details. I think it would be better that you describe the character, as you have more experience in the psychology of counter-espionage. I only know that of the spy and we can't say that it is very good since I am arrested."

"It seems like a good idea to me. What do you think?" he asked my friend.

I started to shake. Any caustic expression from his part could make my situation worse. I looked at him with imploring eyes. And he, without taking his eyes off me, answered:

"Who ignores his own psychology ignores everyone else's. This is obvious, isn't it?"

"Of course, of course," the policeman said looking very gravely at the tablecloth as if he considered some serious philosophical problem. My friend continued:

"Since one's ignorance about one self makes one see the truth always distorted until no shadow remains, I think there is a notable difference between your psyche and that of my friend's. For the aim of this novel, in which the hero is an agent of counter-espionage, you are the most suitable to describe yourself because like this you will distort not a whit your own subjective conception. Naturally, I could be wrong; you saw that when I had you in check, you demonstrated faithfully the quality that I just cited. If I am mistaken, I beg you to tell me."

The policeman seemed to have elevated to the clouds. His smile was so beatific that I had to make a great effort to keep my laugh. He considered the words of my friend with an expression of such gravity that, at first instance, I thought he had realized that, in summary, my friend had called him: 'imbecile'. But my fears didn't have foundation. Finally, lifting his head like someone who has taken a very serious determination, he said to us:

"Your observations are extremely accurate. Certainly, you are not mistaken. My subjective conception is exactly one of the psychological values that have allowed me to have an extraordinary success in my career. As you well said, the great difference between my psyche and that of the gentleman (it didn't stop calling my attention that about 'gentleman') allows me exactly such a subjective conception that the affiliation - excuse the police terminology - of the counter-espionage service hero results in a very interesting chapter."

I was watching him with my mouth open, but he continued:

"Don't be surprised, dear adversary," he told me. "I have been born with a great psychological talent. The truth is that it took me a great effort to persuade my superiors to adopt the psychological method for our service. The categorical imperative makes unnecessary old methods full of brutality. The psyche is an important factor in espionage and counter-espionage. You have lost this round, dear opponent, because you are only an amateur in matters of the psyche; you shouldn't have moved away from your journalist profession."

This man fell hopelessly in love with the words 'psyche' and 'subjective'. During my imprisonment I could hear him many times explaining them to his subordinates.

My friend managed him as he pleased; he obtained from him what he wanted, but he never did the slightest effort to obtain my freedom. And when I reproached him about this, he said to me:

"You are better here than out there. At least, here you are well accompanied and you might even wake up."

Months went by.

13

How many chess games my friend must have played with that man? But we are already reaching the end of this story.

One afternoon, my friend arrived to the prison and said to me:

"So-and-so (the one about the 'subjective psyche') has told me that they will deport you in two weeks, or maybe sooner. He will take care of you until then. I have to go but we will see each other soon."

I couldn't hide my tears. It was obvious that he was also sad, but he was so well protected by his smile and serenity that he didn't reveal but affection and goodwill. It was then when he spoke about those indicative qualities of the 'promise of an awakening.'

I remained alone and embittered.

After ten days I was notified of my deportation. I also got informed that my records had been sent to all the police bodies of the governments of the continent and that some of them, each in each own way, had added or subtracted something obtained from 'reserved and confidential sources.' I well knew who constituted these sources and the motives of their contribution to my dossier, but that is not important any more.

I now see all this period so remote that it is an effort to remember some incidents. The trickery of some men is something so patent in specific cases that perhaps it is to what my friend refers when he speaks about men of mud in the writing that comes after this one.

But the last scene beside him is still to come and what it determined.

One morning in May I departed in an international train destined to a bordering country, exactly the country where I sent that friendly and shameless confidential agent who gave me the wallet. One hour before sending me to the train, the 'categorical imperative of the subjective psyche' made me drive to his office and in a solemn tone he said to me:

"Young man: if it would depend on me, I would let you free. I would have let you go a long time ago. Anyway, once his game is discovered, the spy is useless if not dead. That is all I'm concerned about. You can reconstruct your life in accordance with your desires. Here you have the general outline of my most important investigations in the counter-espionage. I make you appear as the most difficult of all. Naturally I had to exaggerate the note in this case with the purpose of putting your psyche at the same level as mine. I recommend you not to alter anything of the chapter where I expose my psyche. I have camouflaged myself as much as I could. Good luck, and write to me sending copies of what you are producing. I am at your service."

He changed the tone, came back to his bureau, pulled my money out of the safe box and added:

"In regards to your trip, the law only allows you to take out of the country so many pesos. When you got arrested, there was so many pesos (seven times the amount the law allowed me to take). In consideration for the sympathy that you have aroused, I will allow you to take double the amount that the law authorizes. You have spent so much (more than half of the amount of the original sum) in your support, hairdressing, etc. Use the rest as you please."

Since nothing could cause me surprise any more, I said to him:

"Surely into your hands would fall some other spy of a psyche as low as mine. I urge you to use in his favor what ever is left of my money, as a gift from one colleague to another. Perhaps the other won't have money."

He gave me the money, the passport, etc. And without waiting for me to be gone took the balance and put it in his pockets. We said goodbye, but when I was at the door I turned around and said to him:

"I'm going to travel up to the frontier with one of your men. Which one of us will keep this money?"

I had well founded reasons to doubt the altruism of policemen.

"According to the law, the agent accompanying you must keep it and give it to you at the frontier. But in your case we will make an exception."

And he called the agent that was waiting at the door with the handcuffs ready to put on my hands.

"This prisoner goes under your charge by order of the minister Y. He carries Z pesos. That has been officially authorized. He will carry them. Understood? Also, it won't be necessary to handcuff him. Go as friends."

"Yes, sir" responded the agent.

When we were going, he called the agent again and I could hear him saying:

"Surely you would want to buy something special on the trip. Here."

It was obvious that he handed him some of the funds that I had left to future dispossessed spies of 'subjective psyche'. The agent came out radiant, and with the biggest of considerations, he took my luggage and said to me:

"When you please, sir."

The trip lasted two days and one night.

14

During the trip I repeated to myself often: 'And seeing the crowd,' without succeeding to get anything clear except a complete disillusion of the human race and myself.

I had to still travel for five days and cross two countries before arriving at the place I wanted to reside and where I hoped to find work as a journalist.

Upon our arrival at the frontier I said goodbye to the agent. He was a good guy.

I remained by myself in the cabin of the train. I thought about my friend. I had too many dilemmas, which I didn't know how to confront. My reputation was on the floor. It would be difficult for me to find work in a position with the same responsibility as I had. As many, I had been another victim in that enormous machine that is total war. I didn't have friends outside of it. And I was confidently looking forward to the moment I would see him again, because if he had made a promise he would surely keep it.

Unexpectedly, in a station past the frontier, he jumped into the train.

"Have you already learnt enough?" he told me. "Let's see if you can take advantage of this lesson. It is possible that you have to still suffer as a result of everything that you have done. But don't despair. Try to pay attention to that Internal Judge which I spoke to you about. If you do so, if you don't undertake anything new, with time the inertia of the things that you have put into motion will end."

That was the last thing he told me. He handed me the note book of the things that I had noted down, and I never heard about him anymore except when I received the letter that I reproduce further ahead and that he asked me to publish in part.

Upon arriving at the city where I had to take care of certain negotiations to be able to continue the trip, I found the same political situation that I had just left behind.

The next day after my arrival I received a visit from that confidential agent, the wallet one.

"I'm glad you came," he told me. "Here we can use your services."

"Thanks for reminding me," I answered, "but I am tired." And I exposed to him my personal situation, my obligations and the suffering that I had caused to my own people.

"Don't worry about that," he insisted. "Your experience will be valuable to us. There is nothing risky. Also, we will pay you well."

"I reiterate my gratitude, but I prefer to continue the trip."

But he, changing his tone, said to me:

"You are not in the position to turn down our offer. If we would want to we could arrest you once again as a suspect. You know well what our situation is and I assure you that we are not going to allow diplomatic friends to help you. You don't have any friends here, you have little money and will not be able to find work."

"Anyhow," I said to him, "I suppose you are not going to take advantage of my condition to compel me to do something that I don't want to do."

"The country is above everything" he answered.

I couldn't contain a contemptuous smile.

"I know very well that here the constitutional guarantees

are suspended, that you must protect yourselves under a permanent martial law. I know I am in an unfavorable situation and that I depend on you to be able to rejoin my own people. But even like this and all, believe me also that I prefer to get killed before continuing in this train of farce and lies."

The man turned livid. He slapped me on the face and I, that only a few months ago would have killed him right there, held fast and didn't say or do anything. Something strange happened inside of me, something I can't explain and, however, it wasn't fear. It was something very peculiar. By smiling I perceived a great calmness in the chest. The man felt embarrassed, he threw half a dozen threats more and left. From the hotel's balcony I saw him sitting down on a bench in the public square. After a few minutes, while I was shaving, he came back.

"Forgive me," he said to me. "I should have taken into account what you have just suffered. But I beg you to accept the invitation of the minister (he cited a name) to have lunch. Perhaps then you would change your opinion."

I didn't refuse.

The reason for the lunch was very simple. There was a conspiracy underway to overthrow the president and place the minister in his position. In order to do this it was necessary to poll certain groups. I explained to him that professionally I was discredited.

"We can fix that up easily," he told me.

He named a diary of the opposition and he gave me to understand that the proprietors, who were also owners of big interests in the natural resources of the country, would not see badly my collaborations.

"No." I said to him. "I am tired of all that."

"Anyway, think about it for a few days. In my office I have a very interesting *dossier* about you and your political ideas. I also realize that you are discrete."

It was a threat that couldn't pass unnoticed.

I found myself once again in the net of one of those abominable political intrigues of the South American countries, a machine full of lies, crimes and extortion.

Disillusioned, that afternoon I thought about suicide.

15

I felt that I was drowning. I couldn't escape even if I wanted. The police were keeping an eye on me. I caught a tram and went to the outskirts of the city. Due to the people's attitude, by the way they spoke and by many indications that an experienced observer easily learns to take into account, I noticed that anyone that started a move against the current president could triumph. People also wanted to enjoy the freedom of changing owners. Later, once again, they would want to depose the one who they themselves had put in power.

The years of lies added to more lies had ended up making me feel scorn not only towards myself, but towards the whole human race. However, something was changing inside of me and I noticed that my scorn wasn't so caustic neither so powerful. It was something like resignation by looking at the people. I repeated to myself 'and seeing the crowds;' I pondered about it but my thoughts flew to my friend and I forgot this.

Suddenly the vehement desire to pray hit me.

I found a chapel full of indigenous people. I observed them and felt fondness towards them. I knelt down in a corner and started to chat, like before, with a Crucified Christ. I told him in detail everything that was happening to me, and finished saying this:

"Judging the facts it seems that I used very badly the intelligence that you gave me. Why don't you give me another opportunity? If it is possible for you give me another kind of intelligence, one that not only allows me to come out of this mess, but that also allows me to live in peace with my friend."

I lifted my eyes towards the face of the Christ.

I don't know if it was the imagination excited by the desire, but I think I saw him smile.

When I returned to the city, already dark, I sheltered in the hotel room.

On the side table I found a message from an ex-diplomat who I had met many years ago and who now held in his letterhead the title of Senator. I phoned the number indicated and he answered the phone himself. He was very nice. He told me that he had found out about my passing through the city, that he missed my articles in the newspapers and that he had a keen interest to talk to me. He offered to come to the hotel to pick me up.

I felt I had no strength left to refuse.

When we were together our cordiality was artificial. The man was informed of everything but he was hiding it. A senator doesn't look for a journalist in that way just to remember past times in a friendly capital. Our chat, during the trip, was shallower than normal. Finally, the luxurious car that we were riding on stopped in front of the government house.

The senator smiled, like meaning:

"You didn't expect it, did you?"

We had dinner in the presidential dinning room. I wasn't hungry. The shoot didn't come until later, when the senator, the president and I remained by ourselves in a small private lounge. It was about a new intrigue, but this time it had to be of greater scope. I had to go to a certain country and activate there a given newspaper campaign that allowed this president to draw together the forces of his party and eventually of the whole country.

"If it is necessary," he told me, "we can even mobilize."

The idea of a new possibility of war frightened me. But I retained the calmness and decided to tell him my observations of the day, amongst the people. During all this time I was wondering whether they were or not informed of the conspiracy within the bosom of their own cabinet. I let this pass and started to explain that he was unpopular, not because of himself, but because the people lacked the necessary civic education, which turned him into an easy victim of any extremist.

Both the president and the senator talked to me about their deep love for the country, of the sacrifices that they had made, of the ones they still had to make and of how necessary it was now to galvanize the country's opinion making them see the danger of the enemies, etc., etc.

I didn't respond. I felt revulsion. When I came out of the palace I didn't go to the hotel in the luxurious car but by foot.

Days and weeks went by. My negotiations to continue the trip were finding obstacles everywhere.

One Sunday, I remember well, started that orgy of blood, which lasted several days. I heard the first shooting from the hotel. Later there was a macabre dance and during it I saw, in the middle of a populated frenetic and delirious crowd in its drunkenness of blood, the dead body of the president, mutilated. Rivers of blood ran. Nobody was sure of anything.

One night I found a fellow countryman. He told me that he had taken advantage of the shooting to escape from the jail where he had been imprisoned for a few months. The shooting could resume at any time, so we decided to steal a car and together we escaped quickly to the frontier.

Time went by and I found a humble job.

16

One day I received the letter which my friend had spoken of, showing the part, which I had to publish with the other writings.

This is the relevant part:

The Feathered Serpent must fly. When you know what the flight of the Feathered Serpent is, you will know what to do. Until then...make it clear that the Message of the Immortals vibrates throughout the centuries.

WAKE UP! KNOW YOURSELF!

The mysterious impulse which focuses your attention upon these manuscripts is nothing but the echo of the cry which has awakened the immortal essence of your own blood. And by evoking the glorious forces of Life, simultaneously you have evoked the sinister forces of Death.

The former and the latter are yourself, so do not fear.

Confront them, know them, subdue them.

Your destiny is to be Master of both.

And even though you often believe that you have lost The Path which takes you to the awakening, you will never be alone. And your losing the way is nothing but a testing ground with which your alert intelligence attempts shy steps along all tracks, shaking off the lethargy of everything that is mortal.

It is necessary that you obtain experience.

Never ask anybody "What do I have to do?" because that is the most fatal question of all. If you ask a fool, one who is asleep, you will be inviting him to drag you into a dream and with it you will fall into a double foolishness and it will be twice as difficult to wake up again. And if you ask your question to a wise one, an awakened one, you will perceive how useless it is, because an awakened one will always answer:

"Do what you feel is best. If you put your heart in it, always acting in a state of alertness, you will gain a great experience."

In the end you will make out of Solitude and Silence your most precious companions, immersing with them into the depths of yourself. You will gradually be astounded at all the horror of your Dream, which is your human slavery. And, by the same token, your strength to fight back for your freedom will increase.

Not everyone chooses this path which takes you to the very heart of things.

If you have evoked your friends, you have also put your worst enemies on guard. The one and the other will appear within you, and in front of you, in a thousand different forms, and you will often confuse them during your first steps. Your friends will not always be the most charming or pleasant because they will deprive you from everything you regard as stable. Then your jealous enemies, smirking, will display in front of your inner vision thousands of possibilities to elevate you to your actual condition. If you give in and bite the poisoned fruit which they offer, you will become tied up with the triple chain of illusion and of sleep that always takes over those who are naive and do not know the value of experience and opposition.

Soon, however, you will know your friends in the infinite silence that you will throw yourself into, longing and thirsting for words of truth. It will be then that you will feel that "something" flowing, rough or smooth, depending on the circumstances, and the mere fact of feeling it will show you that you are on The Path to the complete awakening.

Because that word, that 'something', is you yourself, the Master, the Creator.

* * *

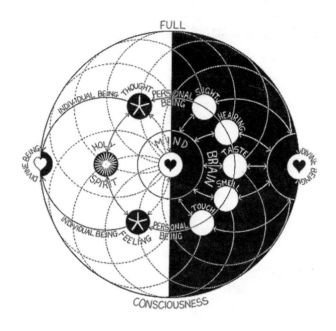

Study this drawing attentively. With it you will learn to use all your faculties to awaken.

Each link in the Chain of the Immortals contributes one grain more in order to alleviate the load of the one who is coming behind, but each soul who adventures in this singular task is an original experiment of Life in order to make of this planet Earth a World of Divine Vigilance as well.

Each man who aspires to this vigilance must make his own track and walk alone, attentive solely on the step of the instance, without being preoccupied neither with triumph nor defeat, nor uneasy about his earthly end.

This is to live in the Eternal Now.

Otherwise the experience of Man upon Planet Earth would be worthless.

* * *

The Path starts in the physical body with the five senses.

To awaken is to use them, and not to confuse them with you.

Until now, you have thought that the five senses inform you about the external world. That is not the case. There is no such external world, nor any internal world. Those are illusory concepts that cannot penetrate any further than forms. But what is real is that you are not a form, and that being Life, you are everything that there IS.

Observe that bows and arrows do not point in one sole direction, but upon two simultaneously. To understand and live this simultaneous way is the first rebellion of the mind. This rebellion will eventually awaken you completely.

And if you go a little deeper into what is trying to express this simultaneous way, soon you will realize that you are not a body, but that which lives in your body, that which animates your body, and, lacking any better expression, I will call it your Divine Being, the hidden one.

* * *

With your five senses, attributes of the ego form, it is not given to you to penetrate further than the surface of forms. When you are conscious that it is your Divine Being who uses your five senses, it will be given to you to penetrate into the meaning, the essence, the spirit of all things, that are also the Divine Being.

Latent in the brain, impregnated in the brain, is that which is called the Mind - that with which you can perceive what your five senses capture and Who captures it for them. Going deeper, I have drawn the heart at the center of your whole life. From this center, extending to the Mind, will arise your individual Being, the essence of your soul, longing for life in the spirit and to worship truly.

Observe that Thought and Feeling connect also your personal Being with your individual Being and I have placed them in the middle of the illuminated half of the Vital Circle, the Awakened Consciousness, because they can be the light which reflects the truth of yourself in the darkness of your personality.

And because they are the senses of the true vigilance, they are the ones which, uniting with what is called the Holy Spirit, establish a vigilant contact with the Divine Being within you, and the Divine Being outside of you, one God but the Father God, with whom you can share communion, helped by Christ, the Lord.

* * *

If in your heart an intense uneasiness does not burn to the point of embracing you to the consummation of your body, you cannot invoke neither God nor the Holy Spirit. And you do not know how to ask, and that is why your hour has not yet reached you.

* * *

"Watch and Pray" was the heritage left by Christ for the courageous.

Watch is to do everything awakened; pray is a feeling of ardent yearning to be one with the Being.

However, he who prays and watches, even though they do it in an imperfect way, will receive generous help and he will learn to receive generously as well...

The help is in the Here and it is Now.

The Yucatan Peninsula in the South East of Mexico is the richest archaeological region in America, which extends up to Honduras and Guatemala.

It was populated since very remote times by the Mayan race; this territory was called "The Mayab" (Ma = no, Yaab = many, that is to say, the Land of the few, the land of the chosen ones).

Also, what is today Yucatan itself has the name (recorded by the conquistadors) "The Land of the Faison and the Deer," a name that retains an exceptional mystical sense. This region was likewise named in other ways, such as "Yucalpeten" (Pearl of the Throat of the Earth).

Note taken from the book "The Land of the Faison and the Deer" By Antonio Mediz Bolio.

Second Book

1

I am the poorest and most wretched of the mortals, but now I have my measurement in full, and for my bliss there is no limit because I have loved the Sacred Princess Sac-Nicte, the White Flower of the Mayab.

I have sighed for her over many years, many generations, waiting for the hour when she deigns to descend to me and to take me to the Sacred Land of the Mayab.

But during that whole time, I believed I was waiting for her, and as I believed I was waiting for her apparition, I was already in reality walking towards her and towards the Holy Blessed Land of the Mayab.

However, how could I describe this walking for years in deserts and mountain ranges, this walking of a solitary longing that only lives when the body quiets itself?

How could I tell the one who reads this, what such walking consists of, in order to be able to receive one kiss from the Sacred Princess Sac-Nicte.

How could I explain about the Sacred Princess Sac-Nicte, the White Flower of the Mayab, and her kiss that is the kiss that snatches men from death and takes them to the origin of their Maya lineage where in truth, the path, which is life, is found?

I have seen her enveloped in her glorious splendour of simplicity and light, as a man who thrives in a valley of dreams, walking along the path of death, would never imagine.

I kissed her and her lips touched lightly mine.

And that lightness was a touch of fire that lit my blood and gave life to my flesh and with its flames it consumed the petrified scum that was separating me from her.

Some time has passed already since that dawn of spring when I remained naked before her, free from the infernal robes that are the seven gowns of every illusion. And when I remember her kiss, my heart palpitates, eager to consume itself in her, and everything in me burns, transforming my being.

She said nothing to me with words, the Sacred Princess Sac-Nicte, the White Flower of the Mayab.

Nothing did she said say to me with words and she wouldn't want to tell me anything in this way, because she is like one sole word which are all the words; and in her look, which is the plenitude of life that awakens the soul, there is light that shows us the entrance to the land of the Mayab and fills us for centuries of centuries; and makes out of men of clay one more measurement of the Great Hidden Lord, for whom there would never be a name capable of describing him completely.

And in such a look, which is plenitude and love from the Princess Sac-Nicte, I aspired to a particular perfume, which emanates from the most pure flower of the Mayab and in my ears I heard:

"You have seen me, you know me, you have tasted the kisses from my lips. You are in me, I am in you, you are eternally mine. You will never be able to forget me, my memory will be your consolation in your solitude and your emotion will bring you to me when you want to come."

Could I say something besides this?

Oh! Man of the Maya lineage!

Make yourself eyes to see and ears to hear, open them,

listen and wake up to be able to die too.

Die completely in one single go!

For the plenitude that is her, the Princess Sac-Nicte, the White Flower of the Mayab, is only found by men in whose veins runs the blood of the Maya lineage. They are the ones who are born to life, who light the kiss from her lips, and that kiss is the kiss of the most sweetest death because it is the kiss of resurrection with which every flesh shall see salvation in God.

You will wake up one day and then you will die and you will be free, completely free to be able to transform your clay into the right amphora in which the Great Hidden Lord can pour over that food and that drink, the only food and the only drink with which you can satiate your hunger and quench your thirst of justice of all those who endeavour to avoid the valley of death to reach the peak of the beautiful summits of the Mayab.

I approached her, the Sacred Princess Sac-Nicte, the Beautiful Flower of the Mayab, in the dawn of spring in one of the many rounds when the Earth also approaches the sun to exchange kisses with him to give him her sap and to receive his seed to fertilize her womb so that her offspring, the Moon, may also eat from such love.

And it is the sap that the Earth gives us, and the seed the sun provides is what makes us understand Man, and gives life to the Moon, and serves and worships all that which was left to us as a heritage by every Son of Man, be it from the Mayab, be it from Bethlehem which is the House of Bread; be it from the elevated Mountain Sinai, be it born under the shade of the sacred tree of Bo...

This is the heritage of *understanding*.

And the Sacred Princess Sac-Nicte is a lover that gives in love, and the mother that offers her breast for those who want to be suckled by her. Without this love, nobody shall see the Princess Sac-Nicte, the White Flower of the Mayab, because love is the strength that she gives to a man in love with her charms and who makes himself at the service of the Mayab.

The night before her kiss, I was in darkness looking like a lost child looks for its mother when it is hungry. And I wanted to take hold of the thread that would give me certainty and strength to be able to walk. And I called for her saying: Come! Come! Come!... But the Mother Earth had pity on me and plunged me into a profound sleep...

And from this sleep the heart woke me up with its violent throbs of longing and as I woke up I noticed a strange perfume that overwhelmed my emotions because I had the intuition that it was her perfume, the Sacred Princess Sac-Nicte, the White Flower of the Mayab.

I, a poor and wretched mortal, drove away the sleep from my eyes and tuned my ears...

And I looked towards the summits of the Andean Mountains and made out its silhouette lost in darkness. A piece of the moon was approaching to suck in the breast of the Earth. However, everything was still dark, but everything was palpitating in the great silence. The clarity of the first dawn, that silver reflection which precedes the light illuminated the summit of the mountains little by little. From the branches of the trees I saw some silent birds taking off in a flight. There wasn't a chirping in them yet, and even the animals were waking up to worship the light.

Only man slept.

And in that gathering which unifies life when the soul of the Sacred Earth is preparing to take the seed from the Sun, the spasm of bliss was also silent.

Only man was agitated.

I gathered myself in the silence of myself, knowing myself to be a beggar of such communion to which no one could aspire except the daring one in whom burns the blood of the Maya men.

And the light appeared...

Yet, a little sadness palpitated in this wretched heart of clay, because I felt the fire and I knew I was dying forever in that instant, but I was dying joyfully because I wanted to die...

Then, she, the most beautiful amongst all the beautiful, the Sacred Princess Sac-Nicte, the White Flower of the Mayab, showed her lips so that I would kiss them and her loving smile lit me up only when the last drop of fear and sadness had died in my heart of clay.

Then, the earth nourished itself from the Sun; I nourished myself from the fire of love.

The heart of clay was opened and the fire baked it and made out of it an amphora for the Great Hidden Lord and the lips of the Princess Sac-Nicte blew into the clay and made out of it a shape with her ineffable breath of Eternity.

In that instant I felt her kiss. And in that instant, life began to vibrate truly in everything I set my eyes upon, because it was I, who in my heart was saying, was looking, and that which I was saying was the sweet voice of my Princess Sac-Nicte, the White Flower of the Mayab, who does not talk or say with words because she is all the words at the same time.

The birds broke out in their unison singing, giving food to my soul when the light shone upon them above the Andean Mountains. The leaves from the trees made themselves the voice of life always mature and green, and each one of them was like me, transitory and eternal at the same time, and above the summits of the Andean Mountains I saw how darkness ran away when the light arrived.

What happened after?

I couldn't say it even if I wanted. Nobody can say it with truth, because those are the words that can only be pronounced with her kisses, my Sacred Princess Sac-Nicte, the White Flower of the Mayab, and her kiss is the sacred word of the Mayab that is all the words at the same time.

However, I can say that in such an instant dies the man of clay when in his veins runs the burning blood of the Maya lineage.

And, understand for what and why he was made in the image and likeness of his creator.

Also know that from that moment on, he will live anointed to the Mayab without being able to ignore or forget his understanding; and that the worlds, men, the stars, the suns, will pass, but the Mayab word which is HIS word, will never pass.

If you are a man of the Maya lineage, behold that I now speak that word in the depth of your heart, so that the eternally Beautiful and Sacred Princess Sac-Nicte also speaks to you with her kiss and that your clay and your water are baked, so that when the water evaporates and the dust of your clay returns to dust, your living amphora in the love of the Great Hidden Lord remains.

So that the prophecy of the Sacred Chilam Balam of Chumayel is fulfilled which says: "It is not in sight, everything that there is within, neither what is going to be explained. The ones who know come from a great lineage of ours, the Maya men. They will know what this means when they read it. And then they will see it and then they will explain it."

And in this way it will also be fulfilled in you the sacred prophecy of the Mayab of Jesus and the day will come in which you will know that "It is not you who speaks, but the spirit of your Father who speaks *in* you."

2

Alas! For many, the kiss of the Sacred Princess Sac-Nicte marks the end of their troubles.

And in the warmth of her memory they find shelter in the winter of their life of clay.

For me, however, her kiss was the beginning of an infinite path in eternity.

And perhaps that is why it was only a fleeting kiss so that I would continue walking, looking for her along all paths of the Mayab.

I realize well that for the many, all this is a dream and it is crazy.

However, the many are men of clay and my lineage is Maya.

And they say these things for men whose blood is Maya.

Although now, you may not understand fully what is written here, one day you will know, comprehend, read, and you will understand me, what I want to say, because the Mayab is one and it has many names and the Universe is one and it has many forms.

And the Mayab has given many children and has made many men truly in the image and likeness of their creator.

That is why I assure you that I am the poorest and most wretched among mortals because nothing is mine and everything is of the Mayab.

However, I have also written that I have my amphora full

and filled with a sacred bliss that I would not be able to lose, even if I wanted to lose it, because it is the bliss of the Mayab and I would always be walking with the Sacred Princess Sac-Nicte, although, at times it may happen that my eyes do not see her.

I would continue walking with her, because only with her and in her am I awake.

And in the rapture of such an exceptional wakefulness, now I would like to pour some justice as it has been given to me to know.

I assure you that I am the poorest and most wretched of mortals, that I have nothing that I could call mine, and even this life I have, has also been given to me, but it only concerns me why and for what it was given to me.

I would like to speak to you about Judas, the man of Kariot, the one you have cursed many times, but who was a beloved brother of that Son of Man whose name was Jesus and who was also the son of the Mayab.

My story and my account begins with an impulse that spoke in my heart, modulating words so clear and precise, just as the ones you modulate in the ear of the beings you love; they were words borne from the kiss of the Sacred Princess Sac-Nicte.

I beg you to pay attention to me.

I know well that all I'm going to say to you from now on, in this determination for justice, is in open contradiction to everything you believed to be true of what happened in very remote times to a Son of Man, Jesus of Nazareth, handiwork of the Mayab, that existed in another continent and who also walked amongst men of clay looking for those who wanted to make themselves of the sacred lineage of the Mayab. For he loved the Sacred Princess Sac-Nicte and spread her kiss in very holy and sacred words that is also why he was killed by the *suckers* of his time.

Jesus of Nazareth was born with a blood that was also the blood of Maya men, which is the universal blood, joining blood, and it is burning blood that in its heat says: "I am the unity, I am."

He was born in a house, the same as every house of the Mayab and in a place which, in its words said Bethlehem, but when explained is and means the House of Bread, the Bread from which even the Sun eats its Bread.

He showed the path towards the lips of the Princess Sac-Nicte's kiss which is the bread of all life, and because there were *suckers* who did not want to be amphoras of the Great Hidden Lord, to whom Jesus called Father, they killed his body on a cross and put it up on the mountain of the skulls.

The men of clay, who lived in the clay, getting one another muddy, thrive far away from the true Mayab of that continent and that is why the *suckers* could never understand that which Jesus of Nazareth used to say:

"I want mercy and not sacrifice."

And could there be understanding in a brain where love does not make its nest?

Oh! You, along whose veins runs the burning blood of the Maya lineage and who would also like to be a son of the Mayab, pure amphora of the Great Hidden Lord.

Before all, learn to be Just, to reach the kiss of the Sacred Princess Sac-Nicte, and that kiss will kindle in you the light so that you know the Father of every Land of the Mayab.

Jesus of Nazareth, in whom the Living Christ palpitated, the sacred spirit of the Mayab, said to the men of his time and of all times, that all their sins will be forgiven, even those committed against the Son of Man, but that the ones against the Holy Spirit, which is the Sacred Word of the Mayab, will never be forgiven.

During two thousand years there are many who have sinned against the Holy Spirit believing that with it they were doing Justice to the Son of Man, and they even persecuted other men forgetting what Jesus said as he died on the cross:

"Father, forgive them for they know not what they do."

Due to his Mercy, which is the Mercy of the Mayab, this forgiveness reaches all those who in reality do not know what they do and therefore it reaches you also, because it is not your fault to have made a mistake and sinned against that other man of the Mayab, born in the far lands of Kariot, and whose body and whose life of clay was known by the name of Judas.

However, bear in mind, you men who are of the blood of the Maya lineage, that any injustice, any lack of Mercy is a sin against the Holy Spirit which is the Sacred Spirit in the Word of the Mayab.

Remember it and read it.

I, the poorest and most wretched amongst mortals, I will relate to you what I know about Judas, the man of Kariot.

3

When the warmth of the kiss of the Sacred Princess Sac-Nicte stayed in my heart, when the burning of life she gave me impelled me to follow my path to the Mayab, when I closed my eyes and my ears to the things of clay to listen to her, in my heart vibrated a singular message with an equally singular insistence, and it urged me:

"Help to spread the light upon Judas, the man of Kariot, for man to be able to make the bridge with which to cross the path of Peter to the path of John and then give himself to the kiss of the Sacred Princess Sac-Nicte."

Oh! I, the poorest and most wretched of mortals, I must now confess that I did not understand such an imperative order and I was pleading for light from my adored Princess Sac-Nicte.

And it was given to me to notice that in such an order there was a strange flavour of eternity.

As if the infinite and inexhaustible strength of the Holy and True Justice of the Mayab insisted, in that, this obscure passage of the life of the living Christ in Jesus on the earth was clarified for the understanding of the Maya men.

And, it was also given to me to understand that I, the poorest and most wretched of mortals, could not be the only one to whom this impulse of the Mayab had reached, because there should have been many other men who, like me, have made of the kiss of the Sacred Princess Sac-Nicte the beginning and not the end of their love for the Sacred World of the Mayab.

And looking for it in thousands of different ways, I found that many men whose blood is Maya, and many more who are only of clay, had written and said many words that talk about Judas, the man of Kariot.

Some say that he was a son of the Mayab, others say no, that he was only a man of clay, who covered his remembrance with mud by committing a horrendous treason.

Since I live from the kiss of my Sacred Princess Sac-Nicte and she says to me that which is necessary for my heart to hear, I will tell you what I have seen with the eyes that are only made by the Maya blood, and what I have heard with the ears of the Maya flesh about this man called Judas, born in Kariot.

I only know that which my beloved Princess Sac-Nicte

wants me to know and I am not interested, nor do I want to know anymore than that, because the only real thing that there is for me is that kiss which illuminates the path towards the Mayab, beyond the summits of the Andean Mountains.

And that is why I know that destiny is not, and it has never been, in the hands of men but in the Will of The Great Hidden Lord in the Highest and Most Sacred of the Mayab, beyond the summits of the Andean Mountains.

This sweet kiss of my Princess Sac-Nicte taught me that destiny and the spirit is the same thing.

For the many, who are only men of clay, destiny is that which occurs in time between the cradle and the grave.

But it happens that, by the will of the Great Hidden Lord, for some there is also the path which goes from the grave to the cradle, and that is why it is important to help shed light upon Judas, the man of Kariot.

What path, what grave and what cradle do I mean? This is something that a man whose blood is Maya will be able to understand and know, if he looks for the kiss of the Princess Sac-Nicte.

He who believes that destiny is that which takes place in time between the cradle and the grave diminishes himself, knows nothing about time and less about life.

And he can neither affirm that he has any destiny, even though he believes the opposite.

He is a man of clay, thinks about things of clay and for that reason he will return to the clay.

Since, he does not bake himself in the fire of the Sacred Princess Sac-Nicte to be a cleaned amphora for the Great Hidden Lord the Highest and Sacred Mayab.

And, certainly he who tries to explain destiny as that which occurs in time between the cradle and the grave, will be able to explain absolutely nothing neither real nor true, because he will confuse the breath of life, and the inhaling and exhaling of the Earth, with the truth of human existence.

Oh! Man who reads and in whose veins perhaps runs the Maya blood.

Think, ponder, inquire about the truth of destiny that is devised in the Sacred Kingdom of the Mayab, beyond the summits of the Andean Mountains, and its light will also shine in your heart.

Think in the Light, feel its Love and ponder that such light has a power which says about itself, *I*.

And such *I* will grow in you and its fire will melt the legion of demons which, at every foolishness induces in you the sleep that you call vigil, and which also say of themselves: "I."

Many are the *I's* that control you and *suck* your blood, the blood that comes to you from the Kingdom of the Mayab.

Be you the householder, be one sole, whole *I*; that *I* whom the Princess Sac-Nicte loves so much.

One of those *I's* which confuses you so much, perhaps makes you also think that destiny is that which takes place in time between the cradle and the grave.

And it will tell you that destiny between the cradle and the grave is crazy.

So it is with many, with the more, and it has always happened and it will continue happening in the life of clay; because men of clay are always asleep and they have not been given to understand that every man is also humanity, that when he suffers or rejoices it is also humanity which suffers or rejoices and everything that awaits him also awaits humanity.

A hard word to carry and a hard reality to bear for the man of clay.

Man has forgotten that there isn't a destiny which is entirely individual, but he who looks for and receives the kiss of the

Sacred Princess Sac-Nicte and listens to the silent voice of the Great Hidden Lord in the Highest of the Sacred Kingdom of the Mayab, becomes undivided and leaves aside individual illusion and does not look for another destiny: save the one which is the destiny of the Mayab.

In the man of clay, there is only an illusion of an individual destiny that is why he speculates with beautiful words and with foolish words, which makes him only see himself isolated and separated from everything that surrounds him and everything that the common destiny is weaving.

And this destiny is that in which *what is below always tends to unite itself with what is above*, and in this way he lives under the law called *Of Good and Evil*.

For in this destiny the serpent drags itself along the earth and only sees ahead and behind and it does not have the plumage of the Condor to lend him wings to take flight beyond the summit of the Andean Mountains.

Beyond such a law is the Sacred Kiss of the Princess Sac-Nicte, which illuminates destiny.

He who does not look for such a kiss is dead.

And to live is to look for the truth of destiny and not to run away from it.

He who does not search in himself for the truth of destiny does not live because his blood does not boil with the heat of the fire of the Maya lineage.

And in the torpor of such animated death he can even dream that he is free, that he has his own destiny and he may even come to convince himself that this very torpor in which he exists is the fulfilment of his true destiny.

All right, let it be that way, because that is also true. But there are those who even affirm that they are architects of their own destiny…as if a man who lives longing for the Mayab could do something that is not the destiny of the Kingdom of

Mayab, the immortal destiny.

Such *own* destiny is a deep torpor.

And Judas, the man born in the far lands of Kariot had renounced that torpor.

As for all those in whom burns the burning blood of the Mayan men, the Sacred Princess Sac-Nicte has written in the book of life:

"To that man whose lineage is Maya and who longs to know the truth of destiny, the truth of himself above all things, destiny denies him the torpor of a normal life."

And it was that truth which Judas looked for.

And by looking for the truth of his destiny, destiny united him to that man he used to call Rabbi and who was the Lord Jesus, born in Bethlehem.

And Judas, then, newly had a destiny in truth.

For in his heart began to burn also the love for the Beautiful and Sacred Princess Sac-Nicte.

And he received her kiss and followed this path to the Mayab.

For Judas also longed to bake his clay to be a pure amphora for the Great Hidden Lord whose love modulates voices in the hearts of men, along whose veins runs the blood of the Maya lineage.

And that voice modulated also in my chest, the mandate, and it was light, which guided me in the paths undertaken by others who had also searched for the reality of life and death of the man Judas of Kariot. And it was also the lighthouse that showed me the coral reef along which I should not navigate.

However, now, it is necessary that I explain such a voice.

4

I am a man born of clay of other lands, but in my veins runs the burning blood of the Maya lineage.

It burns in all my being and such a burning urged me to ask for the kiss of the Princess Sac-Nicte and with the warmth of her kiss, I become an *I*.

For the voice of the inner destiny has called me too towards the mystery, which the Mayab hides, but first, I had to get lost in a desert of doubts and fed with fears. And the heart urged me to remain calm in all that desert and was telling me that only in this way, amidst such solitude and hunger, would I be able to eat the bread of the Great Hidden Lord which the Sacred Princess Sac-Nicte gives with her kiss to the one who does not hesitate to pluck out his eyes to be able to see and destroy his ears to be able to hear.

Until then I have walked along the first path, the path of the lukewarm, which sometimes reveals, but almost always hides the truth of the Mayab.

It is the wide path where one will always be accompanied, and many go along it for fear of silence, for fear of solitude.

And in that path I have seen the light of the Princess Sac-Nicte shine for moments.

But the light goes out as it falls on the Stone that the Lord Jesus left placed as the first milestone in the destiny that leads to the Mayab.

And in the desert I only found stones with which to calm

my hunger and my thirst, and I was one more sheep in the flock that Peter put to pasture, and I was a white sheep, but I was dying of hunger and of thirst for the Mayab, and I did not want to die this way.

The light of the Princess Sac-Nicte that shone beyond the stone that was my destiny, made my wool black, and the white sheep threw me out of their bosom and took me as lost when I left the flock and I fell amidst crags where the storm lashes.

I had not made myself a bridge to cross the abyss.

Then I did not know, but now I know that the destiny that is in the hands of the Great Hidden Lord in the Highest and Most Sacred of the Mayab, has a path that begins with Peter, with the white sheep, and that leads to John, only when the love for the kisses of the Sacred Princess Sac-Nicte makes his wool black.

Hurting myself amongst crags and weeds I understood the words that the Sacred Mayab said and wrote in that remote continent by another being whose lineage is Maya and who carried the name of John.

And this word is understood by hitting the stone in darkness.

This word says that the word in the beginning is with God and it is God, the Great Hidden Lord, and that by that Word everything that is done is: the sun, the moon, the earth, the stars, man, animals and worms, the fruit which gives life, the fruit which gives death and the words of all the Mayab's which have existed, exist and always will exist.

For the stones change the flocks, but the Word forever remains, even in everything that changes.

In this way I had news of a destiny that is the destiny of the Mayab.

And this destiny is the destiny of all those who find the path of John, a path that Judas also found, the man of Kariot, a path hidden in the depths of man which leads to the center of the Mayab and which the living Christ in Jesus showed too in order to take another flesh with him in his own destiny.

That is why I ask for Justice and reflection for Judas, the man of Kariot.

And it is already two thousand years since a destiny in the Life of Man began which has not yet been fulfilled.

One night in that time, over there, in that remote continent, the living Christ in Jesus ate food for the last time with all his disciples who were Giants of the Small Cozumil who were also walking towards the path of the Mayab.

That night the *voice* was ordered, which is the impulse in the hearts of some men along whose veins runs the blood of the Maya lineage.

Oh! Blessed the ears which that night could listen to the beautiful truths of the Sacred Mayab which the Holy Lord Jesus revealed!

Alas! Heavy heart of stone and clay of those who left it without being baked, for being ignorant of the thread with which the Holy Lord Jesus devised the destiny of this civilization!

But this civilization is not the visible one; what is visible is the one that says but does not do, and that is why its deeds have been cursed and it will consume itself in its own destruction.

For when he mentioned that one of them was going to hand him over, the others, who were eleven, did not know that which only Jesus of Nazareth and Judas of Kariot knew that night.

And in his own words, it has been written in this way:

"...What you're doing, do it quickly... However, none of the ones who were at the table understood for what purpose he said that (Jesus to Judas)..."

Ponder: why such urgency?

For it is well known that long before that day Jesus knew well that he was going to die a degrading death.

Ponder: why such urgency?

* * *

When all this was happening, the disciple John, the youngest of all, had his head leaning on the heart of his Lord Jesus.

And Peter, to whom Jesus had called in his words Cephas (which disclosed is stone), declared his love for the Lord Jesus offering to give his soul for Him, but the Lord Jesus warned him that he was going to deny him three times before the rooster would crow that very dawn.

Man along whose veins runs the burning blood of the Maya lineage: Ponder and meditate upon this scene, weigh every concept because all of it has been devised in the destiny known by the Great Hidden Lord in the Holy Mayab.

Peter offered his soul, but Judas gave it.

And because Judas gave it, John could remain with his head leaning on the Sacred Heart of Jesus.

Even now you can read clearly, written in the light, and under the symbol of the Sacred Heart of Jesus, the burning words of the Mayab which say:

"Give me the shelter of love in your home and I will return it to you eternally in my Sacred Heart."

Man, you who read: study, think, meditate and feel what is written for you in the depths of your own heart, and in this way your Maya blood will be enlivened and you will see fulfilled in you the prophecy of the Chilam Balam, inspired priest of the Mayab:

"For it is not at sight all that there is within this (what is

written in your heart) nor what is going to be explained. The ones who know come from a great lineage of ours, the Maya men. They will know the meaning of what there is here when they read it."

For you will have to be able to read it with your heart.

That night the destiny of the Maya soul of these times, of this Katun, and of a humanity which lives ill-fated hours from which could flee he who looks for the Holy and Pure kiss, of the Sacred Princess Sac-Nicte, began to be devised.

And he will enter to the invisible Noah's Ark to create a new civilisation.

For, before that night, in that remote continent, the voice of the Great Hidden Lord who spoke through the mouth of the Holy Lord Jesus, said to you:

"He who has eyes let him see and ears let him hear."

And the Holy Lord Jesus knew the destiny of Man.

For he was born to teach to wake up, to die, and in this way, to live and to show The Path to the end.

However, none of those who were with Him that night understood this way.

They understood much later, because that night they still slept.

As you sleep now.

But if you are diligent, make efforts and do not dismay, these words will help you to wake up and in this way you will also be able to die and then you will be able to live.

And he who lives learns that destiny shows him many things hidden from the man of clay, because only to the one who wakes up is it given to him to die, to the one who dies is it given to him to live and in living, you live in the heart of the Mayab.

And that which Judas, the man of Kariot, did quickly was to hold his time so that the Holy Lord Jesus placed to completion a thread in the devise of this human destiny which points in Maya lands towards a new civilisation, and that two thousand years ago He alone knew.

For, if Judas did not do what he did quickly, it would have been impossible to have that which the scriptures of John relate, happen.

But this is yet to come.

For now, I will only remind you what that part of the Holy Scriptures says that carries the signature of John.

It was the third time that the Holy Lord Jesus appeared amongst his disciples by the Will of the Great Hidden Lord, after that, his body of clay died on the cross. They ate fish caught in the waters of Lake Tiberiades, and again the Holy Lord Jesus asked Peter: "do you love me?" And Peter responded "yes" and the Holy Lord Jesus said to him, "put my sheep to pasture" and he asked him twice more: "do you love me?" and twice more Peter said "yes" and twice more Jesus said to him "put my sheep to pasture."

Three times in total.

And in this way the destiny of the white sheep began to be devised, some of them, when they look at the light which shines beyond the Stone, the light lit by the warmth of the Sacred Princess Sac-Nicte, lose the white colour of their wool and their colour is black for some time, but after they become prudent like serpents and simple like doves, and the serpent feathers itself and flies.

But the Holy Lord Jesus said even more to Peter. He showed him the devise of destiny when he said to him: "Follow me!"

Peter died like the Lord Jesus, nailed to a cross far away from his people and surrounded by others who took him where he did not want to.

And that night after the supper with fish from the Tiberiades

Lake, when Peter had been informed about the devise of destiny, he looked at John, the one who had his head leaning on the Sacred Heart of Jesus, and asked:

"And what about him?"

"If I want him to stay until *I* come back, what is it you?"

And a lot has been spoken and said about John's immortality due to this, but it is spoken and said without knowing what it is that remains from John, nor what is immortal.

Make efforts then to understand what it is that remains until that which is *I* comes.

5

In this way, the destiny of what now dawns as the beginning of a new civilization began to be devised.

It is the destiny that modulates impulses in the hearts of many men for whom I, the most wretched and the poorest of all mortals, write in obedience to the kiss of my Sacred Princess Sac-Nicte.

In order that they are kissed too.

In the same way Peter obeyed the destiny that spoke through the sacred mouth of the Lord Jesus when he said to him that he was going to die where he did not want to die. Peter died far away from his brothers of the Mayab, in a great city of another continent, where there was no lineage of Maya men who were formed as one soul.

Peter died on the cross, but he himself decided to die with his head resting on the Earth, while very close to him, the sword of a man of clay who only obeyed the Roman Empire cut off the head of the late Maya Paul, apostle of the Holy and

Eternal Truth which the Lord Jesus gave testimony of.

And if I say that Paul was a late Maya, it is because in him is fulfilled, compared with the others, the truth that was also said by the Lord Jesus that the last could be first.

For Paul was a tiger made lamb by the word of the Mayab of Jesus. In this way one more knot was weaved in the devise of the destiny which is yours and which is mine.

And if you persevere, even though you are a man of clay, you will be able to pour the essence of the Maya linage so that it kindles your blood that is now lukewarm.

And often I have asked myself this question:

"Why did Peter choose to die crucified with his head on the Earth?"

"Why did John choose to lean his head on the Sacred Heart of Jesus?"

Only the great silence of the Mayab knows where the destiny of the white sheep and the black sheep is devised. There from which emanates the prudence of the serpents and the simplicity of the doves, and where Maya ears that hear and Maya eyes that see are made and where everything is gathered in one sole word.

I, the poorest and most wretched of mortals, have my measurement filled with bliss, because being a man of clay, the clay of my heart was baked by the kiss of the Sacred Princess Sac-Nicte; and in the sacred silence of the Mayab I perceived a murmur which converts those such obscure words, and so obscurely said at the banks of the remote Tiberiades, into a glimpse of that which directs and devises the destiny of man.

For something is missing in those words, that is why they are obscure.

And what is missing in them is the light.

And that light is in yourself.

Kindle it!

For John remains and Peter puts the sheep to pasture.

But the dove lends its feathered wings so that the serpent flies.

And he who is simple ponders in prudence.

And he who is prudent looks for the path that leads to the Mayab.

And the Holy kiss of the Sacred Princess Sac-Nicte illuminates the path.

To walk along the path of John it is essential first of all to know, or to attempt, the path of Peter, but to attempt it and know it with the heart, for he who attempts or knows it with the head alone is a *sucker,* for that one, there is no path outside the Earth.

The path of the Maya is the path of the Sun.

It is the path of intelligence that Love guides.

Why did Peter die on the cross with his head on the Earth and why did John lean his head on the Sacred Heart of Jesus?

Ponder and judge.

However not many understand the path of Peter and do not walk because they know not that even stones have a heart, and in this way they do not understand the path of John either.

Few are those who understand that they are not two paths but one sole destiny devised by the Great Hidden Lord in the Highest and most Sacred of the Mayab.

Man along whose veins run the burning blood of the Maya lineage, I can tell you nothing more.

If in you burns the longing to know the truth of destiny get yourself eyes to see and ears to hear and one day you will find how to make in yourself the bridge that unites the path of Peter to the path of John and it takes you to the Mayab.

That bridge is death.

Only he who dares to wake up can fabricate it.

In this Katun many men have fallen in profound Abysses

and they have lived amidst storm and pain solely so that we can learn to wake up. Venerate them and look for them in the world of reality, by coming closer to them, knowing their ideas and penetrating the hidden sense of their great words.

I will only give you the measurement that was given to me, but the bridge, you must do it yourself, in yourself, at the impulse you are capable of achieving from the burning of your longing.

The measurement I need to give you is very simple – if you see. It is complex if you still sleep.

For the Holy Lord Jesus did not appear three times but many times, many more times as a Christ, after his body had died on the cross.

For you must know that the living Christ is alive.

And if that which is John remains, it remains due to Judas doing quickly what was necessary.

Even other writings of the same Mayab with the signature of Lucas testify this fact, which reveals that in one of his apparitions the Holy Lord Jesus, "*then* opened the sense (to the disciples) so that they understood the Scriptures."

And once this sense is opened the real path that leads to the Mayab is known and the Mayab gives these men Power, Love and Life because for them, God, the Great Hidden Lord, stops having two faces.

And what is below is united with what is above and what is above gives life to what is below.

For these the scriptures are clear and sacred because their truth is not printed in books, but it is read with the soul.

For those, they shall see the floods from the Ark.

And the feathered serpent shall fly.

6

Alas! As with love, time is impossible to grasp with reason. Just as there are different loves, so too are there different times.

Only he who has the Great Destiny in his hands can explain it to whoever makes the efforts to understand it.

We can only say about time and about love that which is not.

Time is not neutral.

Love is not neutral.

You cannot love the one above if you love the one below.

However, by loving the one Above, you will love what is Below and what is in the Middle.

Time can go with you to the second birth; it can go with you to the final death.

If you do what you are going to do today you will do many things that you do not want to do, and you will also stop doing many things, however much you want to do them.

And you will not have to wait for any *tomorrow*.

For time *is* and love *is* too.

If you understand, you can also *be*.

Love, like time, is in all things, it is in all forms.

It is in destiny as well as in folly.

For in time love makes all forms.

Guard yourself well from the *sucker* that tells you that time is something non-existent, or tells you that in loving there is sin and evil.

Only in the bosom of the Great Hidden Lord is the three, one.

Time and love are powerful forces that evaporate the water from the clay and they only let earth return to earth.

Water and earth unite by the deed of love.

As clay they unite for time.

The kiss of the Princess Sac-Nicte bakes the clay by the deed of love of the one who wants to live, so that the water does not evaporate.

Her kiss is love's hidden fire.

The amphora of well-baked clay is for another time.

In the man of clay the water is *yes* and the earth is *no*.

That is why God has two phases for him, but neither of the two is a true one.

The kindled kiss of the Sacred Princess Sac-Nicte is what burns the *no*.

But it also burns the *yes*.

And man is *I*.

And God is God in the man kindled by the Sacred Princess Sac-Nicte.

The time of the destiny of men of the Maya lineage is not time that is separated from the destiny of other men, because men of the Maya lineage are not separated from the other men, they live for them and work for them.

They are only different because their time is a time of a light that never goes out.

And this time is an immortal time, time of the Sun of suns.

The time of the other men is the time of water, like water of floods.

They are not two times, nor two destinies.

They are time of Above and time of Below, that make

time of the Middle.

And he who sees sin or evil in love wants to castrate the sun, but he will be castrated.

And he will not eat the food of the sun and his testicles will dry up and he will be dead even before he dies.

Pay attention, if you are a man of the Maya lineage!

* * *

Love is born from the very bosom of the Great Hidden Lord, the Highest, who created time to be able to remain ETERNAL and love is His Way and gives life *in* Time.

Search in your heart, which is your love?

So that you are not castrated, and to make your creation virile.

If your love is one and in this love you include all your loves, your testicles will eat the food of the Sun.

Only in the bosom of the Great Hidden Lord is there ONE, everything after walks in threes.

In everything that your eyes see, in everything that your ears hear, in everything that you touch with your hands, in everything that your nose smells, in everything your palate tastes, in everything beats the strength that is one, the strength that is two and the strength that is three.

Each three together makes a whole one.

In this way, all that is made is made.

Each one is a being in three ways of being.

In this way, the man of clay was made, the man of water and of earth.

What is one is water, what is two is earth, and what is three unites the water with the earth so that it becomes clay.

What would be three?

Wouldn't it be then *a wanting to be in time* of the Great

Hidden Lord that however, remains ETERNAL?

In this way, it comes from Above, Below.

However, the man who remains clay, if he ever thinks of One, he does not pay attention to it and if he *feels* that which is Three, he very soon forgets because the work of remembering is very arduous.

That is why God will always have two faces for him, but neither of them is true.

He who knows and lives in the *wanting to be* of the Great Hidden Lord rises.

Then, he understands and knows and lives from Above, Below, according to his time, according to the Katun he himself has made in himself.

He is a small three, a small one.

Then the clay IS, because the sense is opened and attracts the light that, with her Holy Kisses, the Sacred Princess Sac-Nicte kindles.

And it is possible for him to manage the four in order to be able to do.

And he is Above and Below in the Great Hidden Lord.

That is also done by three, but its order does not change.

In this way: the one is the *wanting to be* of the Great Hidden Lord, two is the water and three is the earth approaching the sun.

There you have the secret of generation and regeneration.

And when the number of the new lineage of the Maya men exists again in the Sacred Land of the Mayab, they will ask you for the tree of wine of Balche, and you will present it high up and you won't be killed nor thrown out.

The feathered serpent will fly.

They perhaps will also ask you for a wedding dress, if you do not have it, if you have been lazy, if you haven't watched, you will be thrown out where there is weeping and grinding of the teeth.

For the wedding dress is the dress of regeneration and it is the same as the tree of wine of *Balche*.

Regeneration is the real path of John towards the Mayab. But yet you must know more.

He who knows nothing about the *wanting to be* of the Great Hidden Lord cannot be, cannot do, cannot make do, he is just below, and he does not have the tree of wine of *Balche* and the water of his clay will evaporate under the moonlight and his vapour will go then to the moon and to the earth and in this way everything will end.

This is the truth and it's all right this way. Let this man be as he is, because he is not of your lineage.

Let him sleep in peace.

The one who knows about the *wanting to be* of the Great Hidden Lord and only speaks about it and does not do what he needs to do to be able to live, becomes a *sucker*. That one is not of your Maya lineage either, move away from him unless he pleads with you to help him to do what he needs to do, then, talk to him of your Maya lineage, because even a hardened *sucker* can change his blood if he is sincere and truthful.

But beware of the hypocrite.

Poor you if you believe yourself to be better than a *sucker*, or superior to the one who does not have the tree of the wine of *Balche*!

You won't be a man; you will be a pansy, go and put on a woman's skirt.

A man shows his virility doing deeds of love, not talking about a love he is incapable of doing.

The Holy Kiss of the Sacred Princess Sac-Nicte is for the virile Maya.

Only a virile Maya can understand the truth that there is

Above.

And his virility takes him, because he is a living body of the *wanting to be* of the Great Hidden Lord.

Study then, how the lineage of the real Maya is made.

In each one that is one, there are also three.

In each one that is two, there are also three.

In each one that is three, there are also three.

How is this done?

Maya you pretend to be and you don't know the prophecy of the 16 verses of the singer of Mani, Chilam Balam?

In each verse there is one, there is two, there is three.

The four is in yourself, it is you if you live out the *I*.

And when you know it, do it!

The same is written in the writings of John, the same is written in the writings of the Chilam Balam.

The two are one sole book of the Spirit of the Mayab, only with different words.

And the Spirit says:

"For I am, For I am God."

* * *

For the ETERNAL ONE, the Highest One, the one of A Sole Age wanted to make Descendants of Seven Generations and this one is the Great Descendant, which contains and maintains all the small descendants so that they maintain themselves between them.

If you are a virile Maya and if you are proud of your Mayab, humble yourself in secret and in silence when elevating your thought to HIM, to the ETERNAL ONE, to the one of A Sole Age, which is his own Katun and who made all the Katuns and who also made you, and who made you in his likeness, a small alike, with everything that HE is, even with his Infinite Creative Word saying:

For I am, For I am God.

Seven are His generations from the Highest to the Lowest.

The seventh generation has a Tree of Life with as many branches as thirty two times three, and these branches support the beings, because they are many branches and they cannot climb through the tree of *Balche* by themselves, and their climbing is a climbing of a Katun of the whole such seventh generation.

Slow climbing, painful climbing.

He who in the seventh generation degenerates has a certain weeping and grinding of the teeth.

Living on the Earth is living in the sixth generation, and the Tree of Life has as many branches as sixteen times three. The leaves of the 24 branches are yellow, the leaves of the 24 branches are black; they are branches with leaves of the colour of the West and of the South. He, who joins yellow branches with black branches and by his intelligence will make them green, will grasp the trunk of the Tree of Life and will climb it to know about the Great Pauah of that John who remains, and about HIS Great Love.

How are you going to do it?

Waking up and studying.

Waking up and working.

Waking up and fighting.

Studying, working and fighting in yourself so that you are yourself, so that you are *I*.

Take a bit of black paint, take a bit of yellow paint, make one sole paint from the two and look well, what do you see? Isn't green then the new colour?

Yellow is the Sun, black is the Earth, Green is the flowering of immortality.

In this way you can begin to walk along the path of

regeneration and your generation will be then the generation of the eight times three, in this way were the Giants of the Small Cozumil.

Four times three, in this way were the Pauahs, the one of the East, the one of the West, the one of the North and the one of the South.

A Pauah eats the food of the sun.

Two times three is only conceived by the Pauah who cannot die.

But every man can be a Pauah.

And one times three, we cannot even think about it in our actual condition, because it is a Katun that can only be understood by a Pauah.

All are different times, measured by different measurements.

The bold and daring Maya goes from one Katun to another, always towards the Above, and he is three generations in one.

For his *wanting to be* in the fifth generation, the generation of clay that is being cooked, the Great Hidden Lord may make himself known to the bold Maya who has only one love in which he has melted all his loves. But the clay will have to love him more than the clay, the water will have to love him more than the water, the man of clay will have to love him more than the Pauahs of the North and South, the East and the West.

He will have to love him more than the obscure words of John or the Chilam Balam.

He will have to love him so much that he is not deceived by the beautiful words of the *suckers*.

And this love will make him understand and live that love that which, with his restrained words, said the Holy Lord Jesus was the secret to Eternal Life.

Love your God above all and your neighbour as yourself.

And when the man of clay learns to love this way, the Great Hidden Lord will speak the Word which is God, and which is the Word at the same time, and he will make it known:

I AM UNITY

For it has been said, for the secret is here.

So, know it if you can.

All this won't be clear to you until you have hit the stone in darkness.

The Great Word in the seal of the night, the seal of heaven, said to Chilam Balam:

I am the Beginning and the End.

And to the Pauah John who remains the same as Chilam Balam:

"I am the Alpha and Omega."

The two of them are the same Word, and the two of them remain because it has been this way, it is and it will be through the centuries and many have heard of it.

This Katun has been opened so that many more may hear about it.

And it will remain until the First-born Son of the Great Hidden Lord arrives, the mirror that will open his beauty, Father.

By Your Wanting to Be which is Your Holy Spirit, Father.

So that a new civilisation begins on the Earth, Amen.

To the one who wants to know, the Word of the Father will make him know about it, because for the new Maya amphoras there is this new Katun, so that, when the Justice in three parts arrives and falls upon the whole world of clay, according to the prophecies of John and of Chilam Balam, the Just will be with it, the Justice of God, the Justice of the Mayab, because of the *mercy of their heads and the wisdom of their hearts and the love of life in their actions.*

They are three again.

And the Word emanated from the cores of the East so that there is no West. And it was written in the North so that there is no South.

This Word says again for he who has eyes to see and ears to hear:

I AM UNITY

What is one is your brain, what is two extents along your dorsal spine, what is three, which is the *wanting to be* of the Holy Spirit of the Great Hidden Lord, lies within, very deep in your heart and wherever you want to see it, if you are able to see.

If you understand and do this, you will control the Serpent, which crawls on the Earth, and your prudence will give it its plumage so that it can fly.

They are the Small Father, the Small Son and the Small Holy Spirit, the three small Pauahs, the Red, the White and the Eternal Green.

Guard yourself from the Serpent that tells you it makes miracles!

Every clay that knows where and how to do the war to be able to die is Earth of Vigil and prayer, Earth without thirst, Earth watered by love, which will serve God for a new civilisation. And when he dies in his sixth generation he will live another Katun in the fifth, three times four will be his *yes*, three times sixteen will be his *no*.

He will go from the grave to the cradle if he wants to go, because he would have passed from death to Life and he will remain with John.

For his testicles would have eaten the food of the Sun and his semen will not be semen of flesh only, but semen with the spirit of regeneration.

For there would be no fornication in him and his one, his two and his three will be truly chaste and his sex will be lit with purity.

It will be sex no more.

* * *

Son of the Mayab!
Listen to me well!
DO NOT WALK BLIND!!!

Look for the knowledge of the Maya men, whatever his amphora may be, whatever his language may be!

Look for the knowledge, which arrived again from the East!

Look for the knowledge, which is written in the North!

And you will have neither West nor South if you are diligent.

For the Lord Jesus, whose coming was preceded by a star of the East, said that he who asks it will be given what he asks, he who seeks shall find what he seeks for and he who knocks at the door of the Interior Mayab, the Princess Sac-Nicte shall open it.

You must know *how to be able* to ask, you must know *how to be able* to seek and you must know *how to be able* to call.

For these three abilities there is only one ability: you must know how to be able to think.

Think in the daylight, think in the darkness of the night, think under the rain, think under the heat.

THINK OF THE GREAT HIDDEN LORD AND HIS WANTING TO BE WHICH IS THE BEGINNING OF YOUR WANTING TO BE.

Then you will *feel* his wanting to be and you will *do* his wanting to be.

And you will understand and you will know.

* * *

He who wants to be a master, make himself a servant said the Pauah of the North.

He who wants to be free, make himself a slave said the Pauah of the East.

He who wants to live, learn to die said the Pauah of the West.

He who wants to die, listen and wake up said the Pauah of the South

* * *

He who listens and does not do what in the silence of the real quietude speaks the lineage of his Maya blood will suffer, that, the slave will kill the master and the servant will put freedom in jail and the slave will suck the blood of the master and will also die and the servant will tyrannize freedom and will not live, but will degenerate for being *suckers.*

The asleep clay will dream and the water will evaporate under the light of the Moon.

Then all times of all the Katuns will disappear from him with pain.

Such is the truth. It has happened before and carries on happening in this Katun in many continents, where there are men of clay who have lost the sense of the words, which their Mayab says.

It has been this way before, it is this way now, and it will be this way until He wants it to be this way.

For man *has been made* in the Image and Likeness of his creator. If he has been made, he has been made for a purpose.

Wouldn't this purpose be that which the Lord Jesus said to all men of the Maya lineage: *"Be perfect as your Father who is in Heaven is perfect"?*

Perhaps because Peter died with his head on the Earth his sheep are badly put to pasture and the *suckers* shear them, and from those who want their wool to be Black, the *black suckers*, the thieves of the soul, suck their blood. From the two suckers, the black suckers are the most dangerous because they are ignorants who pretend to know and because of their pretension have fallen and will continue to fall.

Guard yourself from them, because it would have been better for you to know nothing than to know the little and badly they know.

Guard yourself from the Serpent who says it makes miracles!

The stones to build the bridge to the Interior Mayab have been lost and few remain while HE arrives.

But the Lord of time who comes from the East gives the Just measurement and there are a few amphoras that know how to receive it.

That is why for the one who hasn't made himself eyes to see and is in darkness, that which is incarnated will seem to him black, thus in the dark.

And the Lord of Love who comes from the North gives in abundance and generously, and the amphoras that are containers and who know how to pour are also counted.

That is why he who does not have a heart to contain his abundance is always destroyed in the breaking up, because pure white is the color of the Kingdom of Heaven.

And the Lord that does not have West and that does not have South, which is the Lord of HIS WANTING TO BE will emanate from itself other waters, will emanate from himself other lands and he will make other clays who will receive him better.

He has done it other times, and so can be seen when you study attentively what it was in their Katun that the ant-beings, the termite-beings and the bee-beings lost; that one day was and that they no longer are.

Stupid men!

This is only the beginning of a knowledge.

Man along whose veins runs the blood of the Maya lineage!

Open your eyes, open your ears!

I have explained to you the three, and I have explained to you the seven, but I have only given an idea about the four, and nothing about the Will with which continuity is given to every seven that is broken in two points, in two times.

He who does not know *how* this continuity is given, he will not be able to do the Resurrection of his flesh.

Look for that continuity diligently and listen to what was already said about it many centuries ago by Chilam Balam, Great Priest of the Maya lineage:

"What is bad of the Katun, with one strike of an arrow is finished. Then comes the weight of judgments, the payments arrive. Proofs will be asked WITH SEVEN INCHES OF FLOODED EARTH!"

Wouldn't this be the same as that which the Holy Lord Jesus spoke in his Katun?

"And anyone who hears these words and does not do them, I will compare him to a foolish man who built his house upon sand, and the rains poured, the rivers arrived and the winds blew and made impetus in that house, and it fell, and great was the destruction."

Wouldn't this be the same as that which, in yet another Katun, spoke the Holy Lord Moses?

"To the Heavens and Earth I call as witness against you, that I have put you before life and death, blessing and curse, choose then life because you will live and your seed."

Wouldn't this be the same as that which, in yet another Katun, spoke the Holy Lord Buddha?

"Illuminate your minds... Those who cannot of course break the oppressive chains of the senses and whose feet are too weak to tread the real roadway must discipline their conduct in such a way that all their earthly days go by irreproachably practicing charitable works."

Wouldn't this be the same as that which, in yet another Katun, spoke the Holy Lord Lao-tse?

"What is Universal is eternal, the Universal is eternal because it does not exist as an individual, this is the condition of Eternity. According to this, the Perfect by eclipsing itself imposes itself, by pouring itself out it becomes eternal, by DE-EGOTISING itself it individualizes."

For them all speak of the green flowering of Immortality, of how the Infinite always lives in the Eternal.

* * *

Foolish is the man who believes himself to be the owner of time.

Foolish is the man who believes himself to be the owner of Love.

Foolish is the man who believes himself to be the owner of Earth.

Foolish is the man who believes himself to be the owner of the World.

Three times foolish is the one who deliberately ignores that man is a purpose of Love *in* time for life of the World *on* the Earth.

* * *

Jesus, the Holy Lord, was a man made on the Earth with Water of Love and he baked his clay in the fire of Love.

Judas was a man who challenged the power of the world and Love helped him.

If the knowledge of the Mayab is what you aspire to, you must try to understand.

And the kiss of the Sacred Princess Sac-Nicte will open the doors to you and the fire of her love will bake your heart of clay and by her love you will be an amphora of the Great Hidden Lord that will give you that which you can contain.

Now, I only want to do Justice to Judas, the man of Kariot.

So that a new Katun begins in the Maya lineage.

And the Mayab of the Andes be then the cradle of a new civilisation.

You will do your part, if in your veins runs the blood of the Maya lineage.

So that there is mercy in your brain and wisdom in your heart and that you can find the precise stone with which to build the bridge which goes from Peter to John in the destiny of the True Man which here I declare is the living Christ in the Lord Jesus.

In the Name of the Father, in the Name of the Son and in the Name of the Holy Spirit.

So that it be this way then.

And I am going to relate to you how and why Judas, the man of Kariot, laid an important thread in the devise of destiny of this Katun.

His thread made it possible that the Fourth and Fifth Generation talked in times and in measurements of the Sixth generation.

I will relate it to you the way I learnt in the Holy Mayab.

Amen.

Third Book

1

And there was a man amongst the Pharisees whose name was Nicodemus, Prince of the Jews. Maya was his lineage, Maya was his heart, his thoughts were from the Mayab, they weren't thoughts of clay, and he wept living tears. And he was austere in virtue in order to increase the treasures of the Lord and he tried to be just as his longing to make his faith living, was consuming him.

And his weeping was a weeping of living tears, as can only weep a blessed, who is not rich in spirit, and who longs for the Spirit that animates life in the Kingdom of Heaven, which is the invisible sacred land of the Mayab.

And he thought of this Spirit, which is the flame of the light that shines on the Holy kiss of the Princess Sac-Nicte. For he also wanted to be a living amphora to serve HIM, and in his heart he was saying when he was thinking about her: "Prove to me that your lips have not been made to be kissed and I will prove to you that darkness is the light."

Holy and sacred was this man's longing, for he did not want treasures of Heaven for himself, but to serve the Great Hidden Lord, the Highest One, the Eternal One.

That is why Nicodemus looked for the water, the living water that was there in the *jicara* of the Holy Lord Jesus. For he had also understood that the *mat* on which he lay covered a vast kingdom inside and outside of this world and that only by drinking such living water could he understand the Mystery of the Seven Generations, avoid the Judgment with seven inches of flooded earth, die and be reborn.

In order to understand and know man, and to enliven the True Man, Prince of Heaven and Heir of the Earth, it is necessary to understand the harmony of the Seven Holy Generations of the Great Descendant of the Highest One, THE ETERNAL ONE, Our Father who is in Heaven.

And in this new Katun, from the East, has arrived for those of the Maya lineage the Word of the North, which does not have West and which does not have South.

So that it is understood and then comprehended by the brain and in the heart of men of the Maya lineage.

The Word is eternally green, and this Katun will be the Katun of an Eternal Spring for a generation, however, it will leave the heart of others withered.

It is the Word that unites the 24 black leaves with the 24 yellow leaves in the Tree of Life, and which makes the *balche* and spins the thread with which the dress for the Holy Wedding of Heaven is weaved.

Then in this way: It turns into a Giant of the small Cozumil, whose generation is a tree of so many branches as eight times three, and who has the power, the love, and the knowledge of all the planets. That is why they are the Lords of the Earth, but they are not Gods, because their generation is only the beginning of regeneration and it is still from Below to Above in order to make the Middle, and their food is food of the Sun. And he will unite twelve branches of black leaves with twelve more branches of yellow leaves and then for him the Tree of Life will be four times three. And He will become *Pauah* with time and the food of the Sun. He will have extended in himself the wings of the *Sacred Kukulcan*, the Feathered Serpent that man will have to lift up in the desert, hitting the stone in darkness and quenching his thirst with the water of the *Sacred Cenote*. In this way he will have the power of the *Tzicbenthan* word that is necessary to obey, as it is the word of the *Ahau*, the one who governs all generations of the Great Descendant, from the Katun where everything begins to walk in three.

Just as there are Seven Great Generations in total, created by the Highest One, THE ETERNAL ONE, when he made the Great Descendant, in the same way there are in each generation a small descendant, and also very small descendants. And there are also seven generations in all of them.

And there are seven times, seven measurements and in each one there is again seven.

Every small descendant resembles the Great Descendant.

A small descendant is man, and he is in the sixth generation and carries in him measurements to measure times of the fifth, fourth and even the third generations, if he makes his wine of *balche* from the pure water of the *Sacred Cenote*, if when he eats from his cornfield he also eats the Word of the Great Generator which says:

"For I am, For I am God"

As it was in Yucalpeten a long time before the arrival of the *Dzules*.

And as it also happened in Yucalpeten, so too has it happened over there in the land of the Mayab of Jesus, whose Chichen was Jerusalem.

The voice of the Princess Sac-Nicte had been lost over there. It was also due to the very madness of the priests.

The wisdom of their hearts had been lost, there was no longer mercy in their brains, and their souls were no longer eating of the food from the Very High Sun, which illuminates upon all the worlds and which gives life to all suns.

Many were those who longed for, few were those who enquired.

Deserted was that Mayab where there is wisdom.

There were a few giants in his small Cozumil, in that remote continent.

As it is now in Mayapan.

Everyone wanted to serve themselves, few wanted to serve the Lord.

Nicodemus was one of the few.

And the sacred words that the Holy Lord Moses had written with the authority of Tzicbenthan in his Katun of light was burning, embracing his heart. And these words were:

"For this commandment I announce to you today is not hidden, nor is it far away. It is not in Heaven so that you say: Who will go up to Heaven for us, bring it to us and explain it to us so that we fulfill it? Neither is it at the other side of the sea so that you say: Who will cross the sea for us, bring it to us and explain it to us so that we fulfill it? For, the Word is very close to you, in your mouth and your heart so that you fulfill it.

Look, I have put before you today life and good, death and evil."

In this way wrote the Holy Lord Moses, Pauah who ate the food from the Very Great Sun that illuminates all the worlds and gives life to all the suns.

And these words had been written in the heart of Nicodemus.

However, the men of his Katun only ate words and did not eat the food from the Sun, neither from the Very Great Sun.

They weren't hungry, they weren't thirsty for the word of the Mayab of their land.

But Nicodemus was hungry and was thirsty.

And was enquiring.

And, that is why, in his weeping he was repeating in secret

to the Princess Sac-Nicte: "Prove to me that your lips have not been made to be kissed and I will prove to you that darkness is the light."

The light has come again from the East in the words of the North, so that he who hears and sees does not have West, and he does not have South, and that the Eternally Green be forever with him and him in HIM.

Enquire then with diligence, for the beautiful Heaven of the Mayab is always open for whomever is ready.

And ready is he who enquires and does not dismay.

In this way Nicodemus enquired and followed the voice of destiny, lived his destiny and did not run away from it.

2

Due to his destiny, one day he found out about the Rabi of Nazareth, Chilam Balam of Galilee, who was talking about the Great Hidden Lord, calling him Father who is in Heaven.

It was the Holy Lord Jesus who was climbing the Tree of Life and was teaching to climb.

The voice of destiny talked secretly in the heart of Nicodemus and he secretly went to see the Chilam Balam of Galilee because he knew that in him was the Word of Truth.

Weak was the light of the earth that night, great was the light of Heaven.

Great was the flame of love in the heart of the Nazarene, great was the longing for the light in the heart of the Pharisee.

And it was a thread of light that summed up destiny that night, drawing back the veils so that the man of clay could undertake the path of regeneration.

And the Rabi Nazarene said to Nicodemus, and his words remain alight in his heart:

What is born flesh is flesh, and this is a generation."

"Do not be astonished then, Nicodemus, that I have said to you that it is necessary to be born again, because he who is not born again cannot see the Kingdom of God."

And even before this, it was rumored around Jerusalem that the disciples of Jesus had repeated his words, proclaiming that you cannot pour new wine into old wineskins…

What should be changed?

In this way, Nicodemus left that night thinking and thinking.

For he knew at heart that such birth needed a death, but that such death was not the death of the dead, but of the living who knows that every man can live, be a baked amphora with the fire of the Mayab and carry in it the measurement that the Great Hidden Lord wants to pour.

3

Man of the Maya lineage, I give here the first evidence of this new Katun:

Take towards the True Man the Sun he asks of you extended on his plate, with the spear of Heaven fixed in the middle of his heart and a Great Tiger sitting upon him drinking his blood.

For Nicodemus took the light of his understanding to the feet of Jesus, and the knowledge of Moses was a painful sting in his chest, for it was only knowledge, and since then the claws of wisdom kept him fastened.

Nicodemus was weighed down with age of an existence devoted to showing young people of his time how one should walk along the Paths of the Lord.

And, behold that the Rabi Nazarene had said to him that night about a generation who will die in order to be born in another one, and in this way live. He said to him like this:

"You are a Master of Israel and you do not know these things? In truth I tell you, Nicodemus, that I am talking to you about that which I know, I am and I give testimony to what I have seen, but men of your generation do not want to receive my testimony. And if I am telling you things of the Earth and you cannot take them, how can you take things that are from Heaven? For no-one has gone to Heaven except he who descended from Heaven, and it is the Son of Man who is in Heaven. And just as Moses lifted up the serpent in the desert, in the same way it is now necessary that the Son of Man is lifted up, so that all those who believe in Him do not get lost, but have eternal life."

The words of this true Man deepened the wound already opened in the heart of the Pharisee, and in the depths of his chest he was enquiring.

"How, how should I do it Lord?"

In this way, his spirit of Pharisee began to die, and in his mind resounded singular words he had heard the disciples of the Galilean say:

"Blessed are the poor in spirit, for theirs is the Kingdom of Heaven."

In this way he began to attract to himself the kiss of the Sacred Princess Sac-Nicte who was already watching him, but he did not yet know.

His heart was bleeding in abundance, for there were many young people who came to his house in Jerusalem to listen to his words. And since he wanted to serve the Highest One, the ETERNAL ONE, in his conscience was burning the fire of death, which precedes resurrection, and in his ears were the words of the Rabbi Nazarene:

"You are master of Israel and you do not know these things?"

And he thought of Judas, the young man born in the far lands of Kariot, in whose heart was also burning the sacred impulse, which secretly lights the Princess Sac-Nicte. Judas had arrived at the foot of Nicodemus to also learn to walk along the Paths of the Lord, which is the Path of the Mayab, and he was eating the words of his Rabbi, he was feeding himself with them, and his Rabbi loved him and he loved his Rabbi.

Heavy was the heart of Nicodemus that night.

Man of the Maya lineage, here is the second proof: The True Man wants you to go and get him the brain of Heaven, for not everyone who says "Lord, Lord" will enter the Kingdom of the Mayab, but he who does the Will of the Father, the Great Hidden Lord. And the True Man has much eagerness to see the brain of Heaven since the judgment has been given to HIM.

This is written in the scriptures of the Fourth Generation.

If you have eyes, you will see; if you have ears, you will hear.

If you still don't have them, by handing over your brain to the True Man, you will have them.

And in this way, perhaps it will be fulfilled in you the prophecy of Chilam Balam, the prophecy which encourages the steps from the fifth to the fourth generation, where "They talk with their own words, and if in any case not everything is understood in its meaning, it is written directly just as everything happened. It will all be explained again very well," (in the fourth generation, an invisible generation within yourself).

For everything written in the Holy Scriptures is also written in you, in your soul, if you can read it.

4

For it SAYS this way:

I, Judas of Kariot loved my Rabbi Nicodemus, who was teaching me to walk along the Paths of the Lord.

I used to serve him as any dignified disciple of Israel must serve his Rabbi, and I was waiting for my hour to serve the ETERNAL ONE and in my heart was burning the love for the Truth.

However, that morning my eyes made me see that my Rabbi Nicodemus wasn't my Rabbi Nicodemus. In his face I saw anguish, and in this way I could feel how his heart was hurt, but, I did not know whether his wound had been caused by evil or by the good he longed for, since my Rabbi was following the Path of the wise of Naim, according to the tradition of Hillel.

That morning, he discharged all his disciples except me.

When he did that, my heart became anxious, and it seemed to me that the omen was dark because I could not seem to understand what was happening. It was frequent at that time to see faces distorted by anger and worry amongst the Pharisees. And Jerusalem was a cradle of confusion. Pontius Pilate, the Roman Procurator, wanted the treasures of the temple for himself; he wanted to build an aqueduct, which would make him be remembered in other times. And in the streets people got excited amidst the noisy prattle in which the hatred towards Rome was noticed.

And a humble man who came from the far lands of Galilee had lit in their chests a new hope, talking to them about freedom. And the patios of the temple were dumb witnesses where his teachings resounded. Men gathered his strange words and were seeing strange deeds from this man that, being a Jew, was profaning the Sabbath, curing the sick, not observing precepts of purity, drinking wine and eating meat with the publicans and with the sinners, saying that he had come to redeem sins and not to condemn the sinners. And amongst those who followed him was Mary, the whore of Magdala, the agent of the publicans, Levi and strange men who fished, a young man John and his brothers.

Strange things this Rabbi used to say, strange things he used to do. But those who loved him used to say at the same time that what he used to teach made the bitter tears of the heart sweet, and that the wise men of Naim, the most learned and pure of this Earth, found in his words hidden treasures of Hillel, and the beauties of the Talmud. But they could not understand his deeds, because for them every deed had to have as a foundation the fear of God.

And behold that this Rabbi had said:

"God loves so much the world that he has sent his only Begotten Son to save it and not to condemn."

Strange words in which there was no fear at all.

He also said:

"Love your enemies."

Then, we had to love the enemies of Israel?

In the wise words of the Law of Moses, my Rabbi Nicodemus repeated to us the tradition of our fathers. But behold that this Rabbi of the far lands of Galilee was not supporting himself with any scriptures, instead he was proclaiming before the people and before the doctors of the Law:

"Examine the scriptures, because before Abraham was, I am."

That morning then, when I noticed the worry in the face of my Rabbi Nicodemus, the omen told me that what was going to happen was because of this Nazarene who was announcing the baptism with the fire of the Holy Spirit.

"Judas," said my Rabbi "You have come from the lands of Kariot to drink the commandments of the Lord and to walk along His Paths according to the tradition"

I kept silent.

"Judas have pity on me," my Rabbi Nicodemus went on. "Doubt consumes me. I am a man with an afflicted heart. I am not sure that my knowledge is good, I am not sure that I am teaching you to walk along the Paths of the Lord."

These grave words said my Rabbi Nicodemus.

Grave, because in the austerity of his virtue, much was what he demanded from us, the ones who came to him to study with diligence the truth of the Torah. Grave words because this man was a high member of the Council of the Elders in Jerusalem, a man learned, pure, respected and loved.

So I held my breath so as not to answer, and I saw the paleness in his face, the trembling of his hands and the consumption of his spirit.

"We have lost the thread that leads to the truth," he said to me. And he cited those words of Moses that like fire were burning in his heart, and he related to me the meeting of the night before, and how the words of the Rabbi Nazarene had increased his thirst and his pain at the same time. And the Rabbi Nazarene had also said to him:

"Only he who believes he has lost the thread which runs through time has the true thread in his hands, and when he finds his soul, he will not lose it."

What strange mystery and paradox enclosed these words?

I protested vehemently because by citing them, my Rabbi Nicodemus had lit the doubt in me, in the most profound depths of my chest, and I was suffering and did not want any more tribulations. That is why I had come to him to find refuge and shelter in his teachings, and in this way to always have a thread fastened in my hands.

We talked about it for a long time, but he was observing me with compassion and he ended by saying:

"In your vehemence there is fear of destiny, Judas. Come with me, we will go together to listen to that strange Rabbi."

And it was already well known in the whole of Jerusalem that this strange Rabbi had expelled the merchants from the Temple, beating their backs with a whip and calling them thieves who had converted the house of his Father into a den.

I protested before my Rabbi Nicodemus, because the merchants allowed the demands of sacrifice to be fulfilled.

"Watch your tongue Judas," he said to me. For in his austerity my Rabbi had put a barrier to slander and he wasn't like the other Pharisees who gave themselves to criticism and gossip.

"It is necessary that we find the thread of our Fathers," he said. "For in those words that burnt my heart last night, the Rabbi Nazarene said to me the truth…"

I could not bare those words. My heart shook violently and to my eyes arrived rivers of tears and I felt the pain of my Rabbi as if it were mine. Behold, I said to myself in silence, behold that my Rabbi says he is in darkness. How would mine be then? How would then be the ones of the youth of Israel? My Rabbi, light of lights, refuge of our youth, tells me that he is also in darkness and that he will not have a precise answer anymore to dissipate our doubts, abandoning me amidst a multitude of strange feelings.

And I felt lost like a breast-fed child whose mother abandons it to hide her shame...

5

We went together, in silence, in the direction of the temple.

And in arriving to the patio, it wasn't difficult to find the Rabbi Nazarene.

Multitudes were surrounding him, and amongst them were also some Pharisees.

The silence we found was full of threats.

Many of the multitudes opened the way so that my Rabbi Nicodemus could come forward, since everyone knew him and esteemed him as a man of virtue and knowledge.

And I saw the Rabbi Nazarene.

He laid his eyes on us in silence. And in them shone a strange glow, but his face was serene and strong, and when he looked at me, I thought I noticed a special message which his soul was sending me, and I felt that in such a look, he was greeting me with a welcome like one given only by someone who has been separated for a long time from the being he loves.

There was happiness in my heart, but my thoughts remained disturbed.

I knew in an instant that soon this strange man would be my Rabbi and that I would also sit at his feet to drink from his words. Then I felt an acute pain in the heart, for this meant that I would have to leave my Rabbi Nicodemus to go after this strange prophet who came from the far Galilee, from where nothing good could come.

There was even more anguish in my heart. An hour ago my Rabbi had left me like an abandoned child to its own darkness, I had lost the thread I thought to find at his feet. And behold that the Nazarene was giving me a silent welcome, and for an instant, I thought I was going to get lost in him and with him.

It was only one look, but it showed me a destiny that expanded in a strange way, impossible to describe in words. I had the intuition of a destiny that did not run length wise, neither height wise nor width wise, but that it made out of these three measurements a different measurement in which all the others were. And it was a strange world in which I felt lost.

Since, for an instant, it wasn't me but the Rabbi who was looking at me, and I felt fear and my heart was disturbed, and then I became myself again and I looked at him.

He also looked at me, and this time his soul smiled within me and I felt lost.

It was a strange experience that morning.

I turned my eyes towards my Rabbi Nicodemus to implore his help, but he had already gone away from me, he was listening to someone who was explaining to him the incident of the moment. However, I would have sworn that we had all been living in that place for centuries.

"Answer then" said a Pharisee to the Nazarene.

My eyes remained fixed on the strange Rabbi, I saw him drawing a circle on the ground with the tip of his toes, and in it he encircled the woman that was next to him and whom I had not yet noticed. The woman was suffering from shame, but the circle that the Rabbi had traced on the ground encircled her too. And even now I would swear that no-one would have been able to penetrate it.

The environment was tense, full of threats. And I was getting ready to defend the Nazarene because I heard behind my back words of impatience and wickedness, and he calmed me with his serene look and in the same way that an instant earlier he agitated my heart, now he was calming it. I remained still, in peace, waiting.

The Nazarene, fixing his eyes on the Pharisees said:

"If you have caught her in the act and you have evidence of her adultery, I say to you: stone her according to the law."

A murmur of nervousness and of triumph ran through the multitudes. The woman was shaking from fear, and from her eyes fell two tears to the feet of the man whose words had vibrated fully and gently amongst the multitudes. However the murmur soon died out because the Rabbi Nazarene looked at them again and silenced them.

"However, let he who amongst you considers himself free of sin throw the first stone."

Great and frightening was the silence that followed these words, because in the hearts of many Jews sin was always alive, and daily they had to attend the rites of purification to be cleaned according to the tradition. And they were aware in themselves that the rites of purity were not always fulfilled, as they should have been. No one dared to say that he was pure and clean of sin. However, those Nazarene's words had been a dagger encrusted in living flesh, and the hatred showed in the faces of the men and of the Pharisees, for great is human weakness, and it is always better and more comfortable to see someone else's sin and to ignore one's own. It is easy to feel virtuous before the impure, to love virtue, to give fulfillment to the scriptures and not to clean bad thoughts from our own heart. This is what our Rabbi Nicodemus had told us, such was his virtue, such was his austerity. And I felt then how destiny was being devised for times to come, and why the heart of my Rabbi Nicodemus had been disturbed the night before. Now mine also has been disturbed, and I knew without words that the Rabbi Nazarene had the power of the truth, and in him had been united the grace and the law…

The crowd disbanded quickly, and with it left Nicodemus, pondering, overwhelmed by the new premonitions that his face denounced. I remained alone in front of the Rabbi of Nazarene without being able to move away.

I heard him saying to the woman:

"Where are they then, those who were condemning you? Nor do I judge you. Go and do not sin again."

What kind of law governs the behavior of this man for whom the scriptures seem not to exist? In which waters did he drink his wisdom? What tradition had formed his soul?

All these questions were rising in my mind like a whirlwind, my heart was unable to understand, and when the Rabbi addressed himself to me, he said:

"Welcome Judas of Kariot. Come near me."

And I went nearer with fear, but the Rabbi took my hand and made me go into the circle, which he had drawn with his foot on the ground, and I calmed down.

"Rabbi, how do you know my name?" I asked.

"We are all brothers and sons of the same Father for his longing is ours" he answered. "Why then shouldn't I know you?"

Both of us remained silent. He was looking at my eyes and I was looking at his, and more and more I was feeling this man in me and myself in him, but I couldn't quite explain it to myself nor understand it.

"Don't worry for now Judas" he said to me. "The day will arrive when you will understand why you now feel it, even when the passage from the flame to the light is arduous."

A brief silence went by until he said to me:

"What would you have done in my case?" I understood that he was referring to the judgment we had just witnessed. The woman was going away from us, turning at every instant an anxious face towards this Rabbi.

However, I could not answer. Great was my confusion because the law condemned adultery to stoning when someone was found in the act, but I knew that greater and bigger was the adultery committed in secret and without witnesses. And like this many walked free of suspicions and men said nothing because they knew nothing about the secret adultery. And this was not contemplated in the law of men, and my Rabbi Nicodemus had said to us that this type of adultery was only contemplated by the Law of God to whom no-one can lie from the heart. Such was the virtue of my Rabbi Nicodemus and at times his authority moved away from the letter of the law. And he had said to us often that a sin in secret is a double sin, because there is lie and cowardice in it, and the scandal before the eyes of the Lord is always greater than the one that is done before the eyes of men.

And this Rabbi of Nazareth said to me:

"The rigor of the Law corresponds to what shelters the human heart, Judas. Do not forget that, so that you learn to judge with just judgment. By their judgment you will know the heart of men. But my Father who is in Heaven wants mercy not sacrifice, he wants a heart hungry for his love and his mercy, even when he is a sinner, for at times virtue isolated from its good can be worse than evil itself."

This Rabbi was destroying the law and the interpretation of the doctors and I was shocked, but in my heart there was bliss because his words sprouted from that which I did not dare to even name in my most pious dreams. And this man was talking without ever referring himself to the scriptures as the learned did, and even the wise of Naim at whose feet I had also sat.

"The Father Judges no one, however he gave all judgments to the Son. And I did not come to judge men, but to give testimony of the truth," he said to me. "There is someone who judges men and many are the forms of adultery and in this woman's case perhaps it is not, because, there are fornicators which my Father who is in Heaven abhors. And when they arrive to the one who will judge them saying that they have thrown out demons and have done many things in His name, I will tell them in that hour: Move away from me doers of evil."

Strange words, strange knowledge that made me anxious.

"Are you coming with me Judas?" he asked me as he began to walk.

And I followed him.

I did not know then, but since that day I always walked with him, from generation to generation, because our destiny was already devised since the beginning of time.

Many unusual things he said to me, but everything in its own time.

For man's soul rises, spreading his wings little by little, as the light expands in darkness.

Many times I wanted to ask him what he did to me that day in the courtyard of the temple, in front of the adulterous woman, since often came to the Jerusalem Chaldean magicians who demonstrated their skills, but my Rabbi Nicodemus had taken us away from that path. Now, this Rabbi of Nazareth was saying words of wisdom without supporting himself with any scriptures, but he had a power superior to those magicians who attracted disciples for their strange science.

"When a man is hungry he can turn stones into bread" he said to me. "But I have a bread which will satiate all hunger and a water which will quench all thirst. And he who wants to eat, behold that I give it, and to whom wants to drink, behold that I say: Drink, because even in the stones you will find the Word of God."

"I want your water and your bread, Rabbi," I said without being able to contain myself.

"I know" he answered me.

"Who are you Rabbi? Only a man of the true Heaven can say and do the things you say and do. Is there no fear of God in your heart?"

"No, Judas, there is no fear in my heart. My Father who is in Heaven is the only God, and his blessing is of love. He who loves me will love HIM, and HE will love him in me. I did not come to abrogate the law or the prophets, but to give them fulfillment. Fear only lives in the uncertain heart and man in this way clouds his understanding of the Kingdom of Heaven. However, it is necessary that it is this way at the beginning until man learns to see the light of his own heart and listens to the voice of his love. That is why I say that the Father who is in Heaven wants mercy and not sacrifice. What is a merciful heart but a heart poor in self-esteem, longing for the love of God?"

"Don't you sanction the evil, Rabbi?" I asked him.

"There are those who say about good and evil, but know nothing about the Will of the Only Good One. And that is why there is a need for judgment and condemnation. However, if our justice wasn't superior to theirs, we would be very small in the Kingdom of Heaven. So perfect is the love of the Father that makes His Sun shelter equally the just and the sinners. It is necessary that our perfection is like this, for such is mercy. How to explain what is unexplainable? Like a silent, invisible dew, the love of God moves men in different ways, and everything I long for at his service, is to teach man to receive for himself the bliss. I only show the path along the Holy Spirit so that man learns to judge with just judgment."

Very subtle was the difference that this Rabbi drew between men, however, I did not dare to enquire more, and I continued following him.

I had very few opportunities to talk to him alone since that time. He went here and he went there, and wherever he went, a multitude always gathered around him, talking in parables and announcing the Kingdom of Heaven. And with the rest of the men impure like me, who followed him like disciples, he spoke to behind closed doors, and they left with their faces lit or very thoughtful. But when I wanted to talk to them about the words and deeds of their Rabbi, everyone kept a prudent silence.

One day the Rabbi said to me:

"Are you coming with me Judas?"

"Rabbi" I said, "my heart is in you, but I feel greatly sorry to leave my Rabbi Nicodemus."

"You will not have to leave him."

"How to understand your words? Are you coming with me you said to me when you were going to leave, and also that I will not leave my Rabbi Nicodemus? How can this be?"

"If you could have bread and water that would take away the hunger and quench the thirst for all times, would you keep it only for yourself?"

"You well know that I wouldn't."

"Then, Judas, follow me. I am the path, the truth and life. And you will break the bread that I will give to you with your Rabbi Nicodemus, for he who is in me, is in my Father, and the love of my Father lives in him, because my Father and I are one sole thing. Are you coming with me Judas?"

"I am coming Rabbi" I said to him.

However, in my heart there was bitter crying and that night I said goodbye to my Rabbi Nicodemus. And even though he didn't tell me, I noticed in his look the hidden longing to recover the thread that runs hidden from generation to generation, and the Rabbi Nazarene said it was the Kingdom of Heaven and that "this Kingdom is in yourselves."

6

Great and beautiful things said my Rabbi Jesus to us during those months we lived with him, in no more of a home than the love for the Father who is in Heaven. And next to him we learnt that which is the commandment of looking first for the Kingdom of God and His justice, and much was given to us as well.

My Rabbi cured the sick, gave sight to the blind and cleaned the leper.

"Where is your power Rabbi?" I asked him one day.

"I can do nothing from myself" he answered.

His word was brief, his austerity was not severe. In some things the weight of his commandments were greater than the weight of the law of our traditions, and in others much lighter.

Great and beautiful things said He to us under the starry sky and under the sunshine!

Great and beautiful things which man has already forgotten. And there were scribes who were taking notes of everything he said, but they didn't take notes of what he said to us only.

One day he related the parable of the wedding dress, adding that he who has it will be given and will have more, and he who does not have it, even what he has will be taken away from him. We asked how every man could make himself that dress, and he answered that there was only one answer to all these questions:

"Love your God above all things and your neighbor as yourself."

This was the main commandment and he urged us to fulfill it in our actions, in our thoughts, in our feelings, and he added:

"If you do not know how to fulfill this, the vigil of the true prayer will be forbidden to you."

And he added:

"Watch and pray so that you do not fall into temptation."

Often doubt made us anxious and he explained to us then:

"You cannot watch without praying and you cannot pray without watching."

And when we had written the Lord's Prayer, the Our Father, he urged us to get to the bottom of the meaning of each of its words, because our purpose was to sanctify His name in all our actions of the world, because without this sanctification, the law of God would be something dead.

"When praying, do not lose the secret thread of your most intimate thought. And do not be distressed for your needs because the Father who is in Heaven knows what we need even before we ask Him. For HE has also given you your needs."

For a long time these words remained obscure, and there were frequent arguments amongst us over its meaning and over the reward that we would find in the Kingdom of Heaven. But our Rabbi used to read our hearts and used to tell us:

"Do not judge, so that you are not judged, because with the same judgment you judge, you will be judged. All that is given to you to see outside is only a reflection of what lies in your heart, the world and men are what you are."

Many of his words spread amongst people, because my Rabbi talked and said according to what he was asked, but not everyone could understand him. One day he said:

"Blessed are those who are mild because they will receive the Earth as a heritage, and blessed are those who are hungry and thirsty for justice because they will be satiated."

It happened then that men from the Pharisees came, but my Rabbi did not want to talk to them, and some of us argued over the meaning they looked for in these words. However, their meaning was hidden in the heart of each one, and the longing for justice should be the longing for being just, more than the one of receiving justice.

Along the villages there were always sick people to cure and possessed ones to alleviate. And often we found amongst them scribes from all parts of the world who took notes of the words of my Rabbi with great zeal. It was then when he told us:

"Guard yourself from the leaven of the Pharisee. The Kingdom I am talking about is not from this world and I have only come to show you the path and to give testimony of the Truth."

7

At night, my Rabbi kept vigil on his knees while we slept. Sometimes he took me with him to the hills and he told me his troubles. For he was suffering and often used to say, sighing like being stricken with great pain:

"Many are the grains, but few are the harvesters."

He explained to me many things that he did not explain to the others then. And when I asked him for what reason he isolated me in this way from the others, he said to me:

"They sleep with a tranquil heart because they have found part of what they are looking for, but you, Judas, you haven't found yours and your cup will be bitter to drink, but your reward will be greater in Heaven. Behold that a great storm will come upon us all and there will be worry in the tranquil heart, but yours will be shaken in its solitude and will find peace only in the joy of the Lord when the law has been fulfilled. And when everything has passed, my words will resound until the end of the centuries, for everything will pass but they will not pass."

These obscure words of my Rabbi produced in me long nights of agony, as through them I began to make out destiny as well. Soon after he announced to everyone:

"Haven't I chosen you, and one of you is the *devil*?"

8

Everyone longed to see themselves free from the tie of the Imperial Rome, but my Rabbi talked to us about a worse tie than the one of Rome. The tie of darkness outside where there is always weeping and grinding of the teeth, and he added that few were those who could take these words.

Our Rabbi didn't get his words from the Torah but from his own heart, and some time passed by before I could understand why he used to tell us the commandments of the Law, and he added: *"But I tell you."* With this he replaced that which was missing in the words of the Torah, and everyday it produced in us a living understanding made blood, which became flesh in us. On one occasion he also said to us, that the letter of the scriptures was a dead thing, as it was the philosophy of the Greek scribes who used to visit us to listen to my Rabbi, and that they only had life when man went from death to life for love. The doctors of the Law and scribes abided everything to the Torah, and behold that their hearts were dry and like parchment, as was the paper in which their scriptures were printed. And for that reason the day arrived when many of them started to murmur saying that my Rabbi was walking along the paths of sin. Even the hearts of the twelve that followed him were disturbed more than once.

My Rabbi used to tell us also of the gradual walking from vigil to vigil, always praying in the secret of a burning heart, because this gradual waking up preceded the death of the ephemeral without which there is no eternal life possible. He used to tell us that without this death there is neither love nor regeneration. He also spoke about that which Moses had said to our fathers, of that which was inaccessible for us because it was the Kingdom of Heaven, and that it was on the skin's surface as well as within our skin, even in the most hidden of the bones, in all of our entrails, but mainly in our hearts and in our mouths.

In truth, it is so close to us that perhaps for that reason we cannot realize it.

However, I found it and I knew what it was.

And when it happened, I fell on my knees at the feet of my Rabbi and said:

"Rabbi, Rabbi praise be your name for centuries and centuries."

And he answered:

"Judas, never forget it, and thus it will happen that with time man will also be able to understand it, and he will know it and will live it, as it will be given to him to penetrate into the meaning that I AM THE PATH, THE TRUTH AND LIFE."

And looking at me, at my eyes, he said to me with a profound voice:

"Behold, I have turned water into wine. However, the hour is coming in which the devil will turn the wine into vinegar."

I never forgot those words. That is why I can now write them in your hearts with letters of fire, so that it is given to you to know and to know how God is in Heaven, on Earth and everywhere, and how man can be in God from the heart.

That which was the most intimate of myself and more real than even my own name; it wasn't only my body, it was and it wasn't. My body wasn't but death in which love was waking it up to life. And from my own body I must set off along the path of return. In the same way too the stones from the desert, as well as the whole universe, were impregnated with God through the Word, but for man not everything was God, even when God is everything.

In this way when our Rabbi said to us that if our love for God was bringing us sufferings and tears on the Earth, it was a sign of the opposite, that Heaven was already very close to us and that this would be our consolation, for everyone who weeps always has consolation according to the reasons of their tears.

And in this way we could understand the parable of the Prodigal Son, as all of us were beginning to be one. From that I also understood and venerated Mary the whore of Magdala and the publican Levi, for it was evident that in them death was also waking up to life for love, just as with John whose love for my Rabbi had saved him walking along our valley of tears.

And in our hearts there was a great joy.

However, deep within my chest continued burning a secret uneasiness, and great was my longing to give of mine to my Rabbi Nicodemus and the rest of the elders of the Sanhedrin.

In this way I could also understand that the measurements of a vigil cannot be the same as of the other ones. Since in vigil the true being grows and grows and it is transformed, until pleasure and pain stop having reality, and turn only into acute forms of the same substance. In man there are six ways of vigil and six ways of acting. Some are deeds of the Father, some are deeds of the Son and others are of the Holy Spirit, and there are also the ones of Satan, and in all of them, is found life, love and death.

I knew that he who wakes up in the path of regeneration goes from one vigil to another, and in this way he understands that it is worth nothing for man to gain the Earth if with it he is going to lose his soul. And that the Almighty God Father, Creator of Heaven and Earth, for this reason gave authority to the Communion of the Saints through His Holy Spirit for the forgiveness and remission of sins and so that the sinners carry also in them eternal life in eternal vigil, Amen.

And just as the soul is forged little by little from one vigil to another, in the same way the forces that make it up are lost little by little for he who forgets the Holy Spirit. Nothing is gained at once, nothing is lost at once. It all depends on how man walks in the infinite round in which God exists going from life to death for love, and how man knows about his existence going from death to life for love.

That is why my Rabbi spoke in terms of trade and said "to gain" and "to lose," because for everything there is a price to pay, and when it is paid it is known, that which is the infinite and what walks and walks in eternity.

He also said that only those who know themselves to be

sick, can be healed.

And when the multitudes of beggars, sick and poor people besieged him, he said:

"Look at this generation and in it see how they have enslaved themselves to their own blindness. They love their pain and they love their sicknesses. They say to me: "Give me, give me, give me, without even daring to suspect that what they ask me they carry in themselves and by their own right. But they only know how to ask, they don't know how to receive. They are misers, even though not one of them is guilty of their fate. However, you who can see, guard yourself a lot from trusting that which does not emanate from your own heart that in my path, only walks he who wants to give. To these others, as long as I give to them they will follow me, but if I tell them: 'Wake up so that you learn to give,' they would stone me. And the day will come when they will stone me."

And he moved away from the multitudes, but his heart remained with the poor even though he had something to say about them:

"How much sin and how much iniquity there is in those who make a way out of poverty and who shun the path of happiness. That is why I say to you: Few are those truly poor, wretched are many. And he who wallows in the mire of his riches is as wretched as the one who rejoices in the mire of his poverty. Since the poor who makes a profession of his poverty is a sinner who steals the love, which lives in the heart of the pitiful. A true poor one is pleasing to the heart of God and he will be rich, because he would liberate himself even from the desires of poverty. There will be many rich ones to whom the doors of Heaven shall be opened, because they do not wallow in their mire, and there will be many poor ones who will be thrown into hell, where there is weeping and grinding of the teeth."

Those strange words shook our hearts, but our Rabbi said to us even more:

"What man has is not man's, but God's. And the Grace of God reaches men through the Communion of the Saints, the seven powers who are the right hand of the Father. And one of them enslaves man, moving him away from his intimate vigil and it is temptation whose origin is always forgetfulness of the Holy and the Sacred. That is why many are called but few are chosen. Those who choose the remembrance of the intimate Divinity will be the chosen ones, then, for them the judgment of the Son won't be lapidary."

9

The destiny of man became clearer in my understanding. One night, on a solitary hill, while the eleven slept, I approached my Rabbi so that he would tell me the meaning of his words when he announced that there will be tribulation in me.

"Judas do not be afraid," he said to me. "You will also accompany me and you will help me in the path of regeneration so that others are saved too. They," he said extending his hand towards the eleven who slept, "have found their soul and there is peace in their hearts. You on the other hand, will have to lose yours before you find it. You cannot yet get the sense of my words, but I promise you that one day you will understand and then there will be peace in your heart and your task won't be difficult."

That night my Rabbi blessed me in a strange manner.

I asked him whether he prophesised the same for everyone

and he answered:

"No Judas, because my Kingdom is not from this world. If it was, a long time ago, upon my temples I would carry a crown even more splendid than the one of Salomon. However, you will see me crowned as the world crowns every Son of Man. You will cry that day, but the flow of your tears will be like a hidden current in the depths of the water in the rivers that lead to a fountain beyond the summits of the mountains, instead of leading to the sea. You live along that current and along that current you will serve so that others also rise up the river of destiny."

The anxiety that these words produced in me was an impulse, which threw me into inconsolable abysses. And again I felt that which I felt before with the words of my Rabbi Nicodemus, that wondering, lost, like a child who cries when he is abandoned without the maternal breast from which to receive life and love. My Rabbi was observing in silence, and there was great tenderness in his heart and he said to me:

"Soon you will come back armed with a sword towards the world of men. You will go like a newborn, however, don't be afraid of the judgment of men, because your life will be the life of the Father who raises the dead. And remember that the Father judges no one, but gave all judgment to the Son. Neither be afraid of those who kill the body, but fear he who can destroy the soul."

Then, I remembered my Rabbi Nicodemus and his troubles and I remained thinking about him for an instant, about his words from a long time ago, and I said:

"Rabbi, Rabbi, have mercy on me, the most grieving of all your disciples. Just as the Father gives life and raises the dead, and just as the Son also gives life to those he wants to, in the same way I declare you now the Son of God, The Living Christ and I plead with you to give me life and to calm down the agony of my Rabbi Nicodemus."

I remained silent and also my Rabbi.

* * *

Then a great light as man could never imagine enveloped us both.

And I heard great words of truth spoken in the Kingdom of Heaven.

And I knelt down at the feet of my Rabbi and exclaimed: "I know now who you are!"

* * *

However my Rabbi put his hand upon my lips, looked tenderly at me and said:

"Judas, beloved of my heart, what you have seen, keep it quiet, for my hour has not yet arrived. And it is necessary that destiny is fulfilled, and you will help me in it."

And he said to me many beautiful and lovely words of truth without speaking them, and all of them were recorded in my heart.

After, speaking with his mouth he said to me:

"Do not fear for Nicodemus. It has been given to you to know things of Heaven that Nicodemus cannot take yet, for I don't bring peace Judas, but the sword. And he who from me receives the sword and makes war in himself will be saved because he will watch. There aren't enemies of life, there are only enemies of man. And in this way Nicodemus will also be saved, when he has the sword and when there will be no need for it. So it is with you. Then you will calm the waters and you will declare that which the Father will put in your mouth in that instant, for it won't be you who speaks, but the Spirit of the Father who will speak in you."

And I understood what my Rabbi wanted from me.

And there was fire and light in my heart and I knew that I had a sword to give and that the sword gives war to the one who is in peace, but gives peace to the one who is at war.

And I praised to the Father who is in Heaven and His Only Begotten Son who was my Rabbi Jesus.

Then he said to me:

"Judas, be simple as a dove, but prudent as a serpent."

However, my sword wasn't like that of my Rabbi. Behold, that instead of cutting the ropes with which the feet of men are anchored to the darkness of outside, mine had to cut off the thread with which the soul holds itself to the light.

And raising my eyes to my Rabbi I said so to him. I saw in his face two tears which welled up in his eyes, and then he kissed me with love and said:

"Judas, here I call you my friend, but the world with difficulty will understand what you are in spirit and in truth. However, the hour has arrived in which I wash your feet. For that which is necessary for you to fulfil very soon is done in two ways: Knowing everything and why, or being ignorant of the service. And man will always prefer to be ignorant of the truth, and will see only one aspect of God, and in his loss, he will believe that he has known everything. However, you and I will fulfil now, as it is necessary for all justice of the Father to be fulfilled. Blessed be he who can understand that which lives now in your heart Judas."

From my lips emerged a reflection of light which was there and I answered: "Blessed be you my Rabbi, Son of God, for you are the *yes*, there, where I will be the *no* for man. Here I see you like the light that dispels darkness, and I will be your reflection in that very darkness so that men know which path to follow, which path to avoid, in the soul by the light of your love, where, from the flames of fire, my jealousy sprouts."

My Rabbi looked at me again and said to me:

"In virtue of your jealousy many will understand that I am the Path, the Truth and Life, and they will not reject me."

Again his grace illuminated my understanding and I added:

"But I am the desert, illusion and the death, and many will come to me."

* * *

Once more a light enveloped us and in it I came to know the terrible hidden mystery in the words so often said by my Rabbi:

"The Father judges no one, but gave all judgment to the Son."

I trembled with terror.

* * *

For man knows this even in his ignorance, and for that reason our Rabbi Jesus has descended to us to show us the Path, the Truth and Life.

For in the human heart anxiety never emerges unless consolation is soon, and there is no longing that has not flourished, even before it is born.

And at that instant, in my heart was formulated a vow of love towards men of the world. And I understood my mission, the one that the Grace of God was showing me in the love towards my Rabbi, and which my Rabbi had sown in my chest. And even though my soul was stricken, and from my eyes welled up abundant tears, I looked at his eyes and I pleaded to him like this:

"Rabbi, Rabbi of my heart, here I can see the night arriving and how I will have to get lost in darkness so that man is saved. Let this cup pass by me if that is your will and that of our Father who is in Heaven, and help me to endure the agony that awaits me."

My words were drowned in the desperation I felt. And as I raised again my eyes towards him, I saw him crying in silence, but with bitterness. For in his heart there was more pain than in mine. At the end of an instant, in the solitude of the night, his words poured out like a murmur whose consolation lived in me until the night of my soul was made, and darkness arrived to it. He said to me:

"Judas, behold in the name of the Father I promise you that in that moment I will take away the goad of pain in your intelligence, and only the fire of your jealousy will illuminate you, so that in virtue of it, the cup of agony that you will feel when our hour arrives may pass by you. And in the depths of yourself you will know that not even the Father will judge you, and that my judgment will be a judgment, but not a condemnation. For what is necessary for you to do, you do it for me and for the life of man."

I understood then, that my Rabbi and I were united in eternity, that wherever he went, there I too would be. I in him and him in me. For until then he always spoke about *his* hour, and behold, he was saying *our* hour.

And it was this way, it is, and it always will be, for he who does not have eyes nor ears.

And for this reason he added:

"But time is still running, and in it our existence."

I would like now to shed light in your heart on the truth of things, for it was not my will, but of the Father and my Rabbi, what was done that fateful night. And for that reason too it happened that at Easter time, the plan was devised in such a way that my jealousy dwindled the light, and only the fire remained shining. However, not everything was clear, and still isn't completely. For me, the darkness that had to be, arrived at that very moment in which my Rabbi, pitiful of my pain, dipped the morsel of forgetfulness.

For just as man needs the light of my Rabbi to guide his path to the Father, so too he also needs the light of my jealousy so that he does not hurt himself in the rough parts of the desert. For it is my Rabbi who illuminates the path towards the plenitude of God, and I who illuminates him in the aridity, in which turns and turns in the eternal round of illusion, when only jealousy drags him. Blessed be he who can follow my Rabbi without listening to my voice, blessed be he who listens to my voice and in it recognises also my Rabbi, because only in this way will he be able to understand that it is not possible to serve Mammon with God's grace.

The light of my Rabbi made me understand that, when there is light and fire in the heart of man, it will be given to him to notice that there is a path because there is a desert, that there is truth due to illusion, and life in virtue of death. Since being the handiwork of God, God's likeness it is. However, there is a path only for he who knows himself to be in the desert, and truth for he who suffers illusion. In the same way too there is life for he who recognizes death in himself and dies, and he is reborn in his intimate vigil, praying. Behold that man feels the aridity of the desert by the grace of the path, and recognizes illusion in the light of the truth, for if man did not know the light from the beginning of time, how would he recognize darkness?

And since it was his light that allowed me to see, my Rabbi knew about my understanding and said to me that night:

"You are going to see more yet, Judas"

10

And for the third time a light enveloped us.

And in it my Rabbi took my understanding at the feet of our Father who is in Heaven.

And I saw him sitting at the right side of God.

And I stayed at the left.

However, the Father, my Rabbi and I were one thing in such an instant.

* * *

And before my eyes were displayed life multiplying itself in the deeds of my Rabbi, for next to all life was shining in full the life of man. In such plenitude the deeds of my Rabbi became the deeds of many men, my deeds were also already multiplied.

And just as this was the hidden devise of the whole world, so too was the hidden devise in the life of man in himself.

In man, as well as in the whole world, every beginning of the Father in the human heart was preceded by the voice of the conscience, the voice of longing for Good. It was the voice of John the Baptist who straightened the paths of the Lord. And he had disciples in the world, and in man, some listened and others could not do it. And just as John the Baptist reflected and announced a greater light, so too has been, and would always be, the birth of the Path, the Truth and Life in man. Since my Rabbi was born from a relative of the Baptist, both were of the same blood. And I, born in the far lands of Kariot, was born from a different blood.

Everything I saw in the light of my understanding was multiplying into millions of different forms, but it was only the life of the Father urging that man also have an intelligence of it.

And that intelligence emerged from the contemplation of the deeds in himself, by man and in man. Since in his early days he who is the Saviour of man had to flee from the anger of Herod and remain hidden during his growth. For every human being carries a Herod within, as well as a Baptist and a Jesus. And every man also suffers the invasion of an oppressor strange to Israel. However, he will have to look for the germ of his pain in Israel itself, in himself. And he will see the Pharisees and the Sadducees and the legions of lame, blind, lepers and beggars stretching the hand, demanding compassion. And he will have a Publican like Levi and a whore like Magdalene and a Peter and a John. Also, a Pilate and myself, Judas, who will sell him to the world.

"Judas, contemplate the world," my Rabbi said to me, "for it is God's life and there is nothing dead in it, nothing can die. Everything that is life is God, and all life descends to later ascend. God, the Father who is in Heaven, carries all in Himself, but He does not exist only for man, but He is in everything and He is everything that it is. However, it is only given to man to enjoy the intelligence of His reality. And when his understanding is opened to the Word he becomes a Son of God, since for man in the beginning, it is the Word, and it is with God, and it is God. And I tell you now, no matter what happens, no matter what you do, in the love of the Father it will be, for you now know how to sanctify His name. And even when you believe one day that you have cursed His Holy Spirit, it won't be your fault, because an authority superior to you will embrace you with its fire and you will forget the light. Such is your oath so that all justice is fulfilled. For I will die and descend to the infernos, and on the third day resurrect amongst the dead, for the Father has given life so that I have life in myself, and in virtue of such life of the Father, everything will ascend with me, as it is necessary that everything ascends towards the plenitude of God."

11

In this way was devised the destiny of man for a long time. And in this devise, every one of us was a thread which multiplied itself infinite times in time.

It happened one day that *certain Greeks* arrived, also wanting to claim Jerusalem, to worship in the festivities. And they talked to Phillip, and Phillip talked to Andrew, and together they talked to my Rabbi.

My Rabbi and the Greeks spoke in secret. And after, my Rabbi gathered us all to announce:

"The hour is coming when the Son of Man will be glorified."

And looking at my eyes he lit the memory of our night in the mountains and added:

"In truth, in truth I say to you that if the grain of wheat does not fall on the ground and die, it remains alone, but if it dies, it bears much fruit."

These words echoed in my heart and in my understanding, and I also noticed that, just as a grain of wheat, much fruit takes to its death in good soil, so too do weeds bear much fruit in the same soil as the wheat. For, the light and fire are seen together, and the flame of jealousy can be fire and live coal. But my Rabbi who read my heart raised his voice and said more:

"He who loves his life will lose it, and he who abhors his life in this world will keep it for eternal life. If anyone serves me, follow me, and where I will be, there too will be the one who serves me."

He kept silent for an instant, and looking at us in the eyes, he said to us without words what each of us had to understand and do. And gazing upon me, he calmed the agitation of my chest, saying:

"If anyone serves me, my Father will honour him."

"Now my soul was disturbed. What would I say? Father, save me from this hour. But, for this, I have come in this hour."

And again I could understand to what hour my Rabbi was referring to, for his time wasn't only the time of Israel in those days, but time that would be multiplied for the glory of God. And in this multiplication, what was one and divine in my Rabbi now would come to be many equally divine in the glory of God and by the grace of the Holy Spirit. And in this grace my Rabbi exclaimed with a voice of thunder that still resounds now in the depths of the consciousness of every human being:

"Father, glorify your name!"

Then, all of us knelt down before him. And the light was made in us all, and the voice of Heaven spoke in the hearts of each one, vibrating with the emotion that my Rabbi lit in us. And all of us could hear the voice of Heaven:

"And I have glorified it and I will glorify it again."

And this voice sounds and resounds, and also multiplies as it has multiplied before in other forms, and will continue multiplying for centuries and centuries. And in this multiplication will take place the arrival of many hours of light solely when the hour of darkness oppresses the heart of man.

The *multitude* said that it was the voice of an angel, but my Rabbi, extending his hand upon us, said to us:

"That voice hasn't come because of me, but because of you."

And the miracle was done due to his multiplication, just as once, my Rabbi had multiplied the bread and the fish. Bread for the hungry and fish for those who, having tasted the bread, made the oath of fisherman in order to glorify God.

My Rabbi said to us again:

"Now is the judgment of this world, now the Prince of this world will be thrown out."

And in virtue of the miracle that had already taken place outside the world, he announced to us his promise for all times.

"And if I were lifted from the Earth, I will bring everyone to myself."

With this our Rabbi taught us the miracle of all multiplication.

And each of us felt the weight and at the same time the glory of the Law and the Grace of God. And each one of us knew what we needed to do, since, by following my Rabbi, each one also carried many in ourselves. However, only those who would want to do it will walk with him.

12

It was then that my Rabbi sent me before him to Jerusalem warning me:

"Judas, don't be afraid of those who kill the body, but of those who can kill the soul."

In Jerusalem rumours were boiling. And my appearance wasn't the same as before, because I had stopped being a Pharisee. That is why my old friends did not recognize me, neither in the streets nor in the temple. However, Nicodemus recognized me and we talked about my Rabbi.

Nicodemus was anxious because of the political effervescence in the city. Herod and his people, as well as the others, were awaiting the entrance of my Rabbi in the Passover, in order to stir up a revolt against Rome. However, I explained to Nicodemus what my Rabbi Jesus had explained to me, that his kingdom wasn't from this world.

A Roman Decurion, a friend of Nicodemus, was suspicious of my Rabbi and interrogated me with grave jealousy, as he wanted to guide the behaviour of the procurator Pilate. I explained to him that my Rabbi taught to worship the Father who is in Heaven and not the Caesar, even if the Roman Caesar was also the deed of the very Father, the God of Israel was the only true God. The Decurion laughed at my words, but I left him in peace. For my Rabbi had taught us not to judge, and in the miracle of the glorification of the Father for all times, it was necessary that the light fall equally upon the righteous and the sinners.

However, my Rabbi Nicodemus did not understand the Justice of the Father but only the justice of the Law. However, he wanted to understand, for in his heart the portent was strong and his wish to serve the Lord, powerful. That is why he asked me to show him the baptism with fire and the Holy Spirit.

And remembering the light of my Rabbi, I said:

"Nicodemus, brother, the Holy Spirit is Holy because it is invisible, inaudible and impalpable outside the human heart. However, there are those to whom it arrives like a perfume, and for others with the flavour of milk and honey that our fathers ate, those who knew which one was the Promised Land for the Jews. That is why the Holy Spirit cannot communicate with words of this world, because it is immaculate and as soon as it touches the things of the world it receives a blemish. That is why my Rabbi stressed on telling us: 'Blessed are those of pure heart because they shall see God.' Could it be otherwise Nicodemus? Even in the understanding of every sinner the light shines, however, not all sinners know themselves to be sinners, and for that reason not everyone dares to turn their faces towards it. For there is no light, neither fire, of the Holy Spirit for he who does not *suffer* darkness. And a pure heart has to be empty and clean of everything, save the longing for God that God himself sowed in our first fathers. However, it is the light that calls, but a spark is not less than the light."

Nicodemus pondered for an instant in his confusion.

He said to me: "It is necessary that the Law is observed by the Elders of Israel. How then does your Rabbi seek it to be sown in the hearts of the multitudes?"

And I answered to him:

"The Law arrives to men by the Grace of God, for before the world was, the Father is. The same with my Rabbi. Before

Abraham was, he is."

"You are blaspheming Judas" Nicodemus exclaimed.

"The peace of the Lord be with you Nicodemus."

"And with your spirit."

And I moved away from Nicodemus, but I knew that the light was going to increase in his understanding, since, even though the High Priest was anxious too about my Rabbi's deeds, in everyone was burning the hope of a liberation.

When I arrived to the patio of the temple I found Caiphas. Knowing I was a disciple of the Christ, he also interrogated me:

"We want to act with prudence Judas" he said to me. "However, we must keep the zeal of the tradition so that people are not lost."

"My Rabbi has not come to abrogate the Law or the prophets, but he has come to give them fulfilment."

Anger showed up in his face and in it I saw a reflection of that vision in which every miracle existed already and was multiplying itself. I saw in an instant how the face of Caiphas, and even his thoughts and his feelings, were also multiplying in times that were to come.

"Do you mean we do not give fulfilment to the Law?"

"My Rabbi has said that not all those who cry out 'Lord, Lord' will see the Kingdom of Heaven, but he who does the will of the Father who is in Heaven."

"And how are we going to know about that will unless we interpret the Law of Moses?"

"Aspiring to the grace of my Rabbi Jesus."

And I also moved away from him.

That night, I was anxiously watching and praying as our Rabbi had taught us, and amidst my prayers I heard his voice vibrating within my chest:

"Jerusalem, Jerusalem! That having eyes and does not see

and ears and does not hear. And every word of a prophet is stoned in you. And so it is with man in his diminished understanding. One day he will shout "Hosanna!" and the next, "Crucify him!" And in all this there is Truth, and so it will be. Since in stoning there is also justice. For stones become bread, and bread the Holy Spirit, when the will of God is fulfilled. Cloudy is my talking, but my saying is not cloudy, the light in the heart of man shines so that it can open his understanding."

In my agony I received consolation, for I saw that, that member of man was Jerusalem in the miraculous multiplication that I knew too well. And how there was in it a secret fight between the procurator of the strange invader and the custodians of the Law of God. And how in a pitiless deaf war between them was emerging the pain of a multitude of beings who depended on them, and how, because both ignored it, there was pain and poverty in Israel.

At this moment I knew that my Rabbi would enter Jerusalem.

And that is what happened.

A few days later he entered, seated on the rump of a donkey and not on a steed. In a peace like and humble manner, and he was not coming in a battle like manner. For it was necessary that man was saved, and saving could only be done by not making violence, but by making himself seen only by those who have eyes and ears to see and hear.

* * *

Annas, Caiphas, the Roman Decurion who was talking on behalf of Pilate, and several Pharisees had discussions three nights before the Passover celebration. Nicodemus was opposed to the violence that Caiphas was looking for and he sent for me.

And when he withdrew together with the Roman Decurion, I remained alone with Caiphas and Annas.

"What purpose moves your Rabbi, Judas?" They said to me.

"That man knows the truth and is free" I answered.

Both smiled without hiding their scorn.

"It is necessary to apprehend him," Annas commented.

My heart was palpitating full of anguish, for I felt the power of my Rabbi urging me to talk.

"I can tell you where you will find the Christ," I announced

And both looked at me with surprise. And in that instant I understood how the Grace of God was also operating in their understanding, since, more than my Rabbi, they wanted the Christ. That is how we arranged a meeting for the following night.

And I informed Nicodemus about it. And Nicodemus understood even when his eyes were full of tears and in them I could see his compassion for me.

Seven days before the arrival of my Rabbi to Jerusalem I slept in Bethany, in the house of Lazarus the resurrected, and we took the communion together with Martha and Mary. And in that communion the word of consolation from our Rabbi reached us again, saying to each of us in the depths of our own hearts:

"He closed their ears and hardened their hearts so that they could not see with their eyes and understand from their hearts, and they convert themselves, and I will cure them."

Then, I knew that the multiplication repeated the heart of things, for these were the words of Isaiah. And I understood how the princes of the Pharisees also longed and believed in my Rabbi Jesus, knowing him to be the living Christ. However, they were afraid of the anger of the owners of the synagogue, for they loved the glory of man more than the glory of God.

And everything was as it should have been.

For again the word of the Christ spoke in us, in the heart, and repeated:

"If the grain of wheat does not fall and die, it remains alone, but if it dies it bears much fruit."

And all of us knew that the life of the Lord was in the hands of our Rabbi who had come to sow for all times to come, just as before him our fathers had sown with the Law, and the prophets. However, this fruit, new fruit it was. But not everyone was able to take this word.

13

The next day, *the sixth day* before Passover, my Rabbi arrived in Bethany.

And the six days followed impregnated with emotion and life. Each day marked its time in the multiplication of the deeds until the end.

And our Rabbi loved us all until the end.

The fifth day, at night, he took us with him to his supper. And said to us:

"Today is the fifth day before Passover. And in the Passover my Father will be glorified."

And he washed our feet.

However, not everyone became clean

And in the silence which followed his words, when there was anxiety in us all, my Rabbi said:

"I am not talking about you all, I know who I have elected. The one who eats bread with me has risen his heel against me.

From now I tell you, so that when it is done you believe that it was I. Truly I tell you: He who receives the one I have sent, receives me, he who receives me, receives the one who has sent me."

Then amidst everyone's anxiety, when John asked him who was going to hand him over, he announced:

"He to whom I shall give the dipped bread."

And stretching the hand with the dipped bread in it, he offered it to me and *I received it*. And his eyes looked at me full of compassion and mine were covered in tears, for my soul was shaken with terror. At that instance my Rabbi looked at me and in his look he placed the memory of that night in the mountain when he had taken me to the left of our Father who is in Heaven.

And with compassion, he said to me:

"What you are doing, do it quickly."

And I swallowed the morsel...

And when I had swallowed, the multiplication of my deeds remained for all times.

And the time devised that night by my Rabbi Jesus had reached its end, because it was necessary that it was this way for the glorification of the Father who is in Heaven.

As I ate the dipped bread that night, I felt the barrier of time falling upon me, and the eternal, the plenitude of God that I have known in the love of my Rabbi, wasn't in my heart anymore. My understanding became foggy and I saw myself on my knees prostrated before death, dreading, for the darkness was extending in time until the oppression that man suffers in his fall makes him cry out and beg for the light again.

And Satan spoke in my blood with words of fire:

"Forget the light that was."

And I started to feel the transformation.

Then, I felt that I no longer was the owner of my being,

but a slave of my transformation, and fell upon my mind the darkness of the Earth. And what were the reflections of the being of light, shone in it with a multiplicity of shadows, and it was a changing range of colours, but in none of them was there the original whiteness.

And I fell in forgetfulness of my own Rabbi, and I was in him no more.

And still, his light remained burning in my darkness, but I could not see it.

Then, the eyes of my Rabbi looked at me and for an instant I felt his pity in my own heart, but soon after it turned into anger and spite, for with the dipped morsel was diluted all the plenitude that he himself had given me.

I then believed in death.

And my bitterness became my strength.

And I acted. However, I did not act from myself, for, all the authority had been taken away from me, so that he who has eyes sees and if ears, hears. For in these words of mine there is not a syllable that does not say something, nor a word that does not indicate a time.

However, nothing that belongs to my Rabbi is of time, and his words are repeated now as in all times: "My Kingdom is not from this world."

And from myself I add: "This world is in the Kingdom, but not in the way I am. What could be from this world of the Kingdom is suspended, hanging from a branch, lacking in plenitude, without the brain and the heart touching the Heaven, without the feet making their way through the earth."

* * *

Man of the Maya lineage: In three parts I have related what I have known about Judas. He walked anointed by the love of Jesus until the novena, who washed his feet, but they did not become fully cleaned, because in the second round of the nine, he sold the Christ to the world, and the scriptures were fulfilled.

Then, when Judas arrived with a party, ministers of the pontiffs and the Pharisees, Jesus asked them:

"Who are you looking for?"

And they said:

"Jesus the Nazarene."

And he said:

"I am."

And they went back and fell on the ground.

And for the second time Jesus asked them who they were looking for, and for the second time they said: "Jesus the Nazarene."

And for the second time he said:

"I am, since you are looking for me, let these ones go."

The envoys of the prince of this world asked twice, but no more.

And with this the scripture was also fulfilled.

For the eleven were saved.

And in this way the spirit remains in Heaven, the body on the Earth.

Where do you carry the soul?

GLOSSARY

Maya words used in books two and three.

AHUA - God, man-divine, king, "God-King", "Great Lord".

BALCHE - Drink extracted from a tree in Yucatan which is fermented. It also means hidden tree.

CENOTE - Well of subterranean waters. The sacred Cenote existed in Chinchen Itza and it was a place for mystic ceremonies.

COZUMIL - Small Island in front of the Yucatan peninsula which means "Land of the Swallows". At present it is called Cozumel. This island no doubt was a seminary or an esoteric school of the Maya culture.

DZULES - Lords, this name was given to the Spanish in the early years of the conquest.

KATUN - Epoch or period of the Maya chronology. Small Maya century of 20 years and of 360 days.

KUKULCAN - Great Divine instructor "Serpent with Feathers" equivalent to Quetzalcoatl Nahoa.

MANI - "Everything passed". It is also the name of a famous Mayan city which, in the times of the conquest, was the headquarters of the Xiu Kings and the last refuge of the Maya civilization and of its religious culture.

PAUAH - "Those who distribute or disperse the stream of life". The four celestial spirits.

TZICBENTHAN - "Word which must be obeyed".

SAC-NICTE - White flower.

Book Order Information

For order options visit:
http://www.absolutepublishing.net

The teachings in this book can be further explored through the free online courses offered at:
http://www.mysticweb.org